The Property Boom

THE EFFECTS OF BUILDING SOCIETY
BEHAVIOUR ON HOUSE PRICES

The Property Boom

THE EFFECTS OF BUILDING SOCIETY
BEHAVIOUR ON HOUSE PRICES

David G. Mayes

MARTIN ROBERTSON

First published in 1979 by Martin Robertson & Co. Ltd., 108 Cowley Road, Oxford OX4 1JF

ISBN 0 85520 296 3

Typeset by Preface Ltd., Salisbury
Printed and bound in Great Britain by Richard Clay Ltd. at
The Chaucer Press, Bungay, Suffolk

Contents

Acknowledgements

I am very grateful for the financial support of this research by the Houblon-Norman Fund, without whose help the work would never have taken place. Thanks are also due to those who gave helpful advice and encouragement while the work was in progress, particularly to Mark Boléat of the Building Societies Association and to Brian Norris and Brian Sims of the Bristol and West Building Society. The final version has benefitted greatly from the detailed comments and helpful suggestions of Mark Boléat and Martin Timbrell on previous drafts. The initial data collection and assistance with the more tiresome side of the computer estimation was accomplished cheerfully by Julie Davison. Finally, my heartfelt thanks to Vi Palfrey who converted my hieroglyphics into an elegant English typescript. Unfortunately, I cannot blame these people for the remaining mistakes and errors which remain my own. This research was undertaken while I was at the University of Exeter.

Figures 4.4 and 4.5 are reproduced with the permission of the controller of Her Majesty's Stationary Office.

David G. Mayes
University of Exeter

1 Introduction to the Problem

The 1970s have seen rates of inflation which are totally unprecedented in the memory of those living in the UK. Not surprisingly these events have stimulated a wide interest in their causes and in the process by which they take place. Beyond this the reactions and behaviour of both individuals and organizations in the face of these novel conditions provide a fertile field of economic and social enquiry. The first major area in which inflation began to bite for a large section of the population was in the market for owner-occupied housing where prices (taking the average price of new houses mortgaged with Building Societies as published in *Housing and Construction Statistics*) rose by 129 per cent during the years 1971–73 compared with a rise of only 72 per cent during the whole of the previous ten years. A number of theories have been advanced to explain this inflation, and several commentators have suggested that the behaviour of building societies was a prime cause. The *prima facie* evidence for these suggestions is that between the beginning of 1970 and the summer of 1972 the value of mortgage advances by building societies increased by 166 per cent. The building society movement has, as one might expect, vigorously denied responsibility and has argued that its increased lending was in response to increased demand. This book examines the validity of these arguments in the light of the evidence available now and suggests what the real causes of the inflation were.

Clearly the solution of this problem is no easy task as it requires an explanation not only of the behaviour of the housing market but of the behaviour of building societies as well. The structure of this analysis is therefore to begin by setting out, in Chapter 2, the nature of the housing market in the UK. Although over 50 per cent of all dwellings in the UK are now owner-occupied, owner-occupation is only one form of tenure of a dwelling among several. The price of private houses will be

1

affected by activities in other sectors of the housing market, since one form of tenure can always be a substitute for another. Thus an increase in the level of local authority rents, for example, will increase the demand for owner-occupied housing if other factors remain unchanged. Secondly, the form of tenure of any particular dwelling is not irrevocable. In recent years the government has encouraged local authorities to sell some of their houses to sitting tenants, and much more importantly there has been a fairly rapid contraction in the privately rented sector for both furnished and unfurnished dwellings. Thus there can be considerable changes in the supply of private houses irrelevant of the rate of construction or demolition of existing dwellings.

The explanation of new construction itself has been the subject of many enquiries in the past, both in the UK and in other countries, so there is substantial literature to draw upon to explain recent trends and behaviour. The most striking feature in the analysis of the level of housebuilding over time is the existence of substantial cycles. While these cycles are related to the overall level of economic activity in the country much of the variation remains to be explained. It might be expected that not only is the demand for private houses affected by their price, but their supply is also. However, houses cannot be supplied immediately, and hence there will be a complex lag relation between the number of houses actually completed in a particular time period and the numbers begun or under construction in previous periods. This relation will not necessarily be symmetric, for while it is readily possible to work on a house which is being built, completed houses cannot be obtained immediately. Hence an increase in completions is dependent upon either a prior increase in starts or a reduction in the number of houses in progress.

The most important factor in the development of the housing market is, however, government policy itself. Successive governments have sought to regulate and control housing, with legislation controlling permission to build, standards of construction, the level of rents in both the private and public sectors, security of tenure and the amounts of income tax deductible for interest payments on mortgages. Some of these measures have been contradictory and others have led to results very different from those intended. Particular emphasis is therefore laid, in Chapter 2, on the rôle of government intervention in the market and its implications for the supply and demand for owner-occupied housing.

Without the existence of credit institutions specializing in the provision of mortgages for home ownership, the size of the owner-occupied sector would be much smaller. Finance is provided by building societies, local authorities, insurance companies, banks and a number of other smaller lenders; but of these institutions, building societies were providing 85 per cent of available funds in 1973, so their influence on the market is very substantial. Chapter 3 is devoted to a consideration of the way in which building societies provide housing finance. The provision of this finance is dependent in turn upon the funds which the building societies can themselves borrow. The general behaviour of building societies both as lenders and borrowers has to be explained as does their position in the financial sector as a whole. Building societies are not profit-making concerns, and their behaviour cannot necessarily be explained in the same way as that of other commercial financial intermediaries. Their primary purpose is to make as large a quantity of funds available for house purchase as can be maintained stably. Traditionally the societies also provide a safe and convenient service to the small saver, many of whom may be potential customers for mortgages. It is thus necessary to determine what it is that building societies are trying to achieve before their effects on the housing market can be examined successfully.

Having considered both the housing market and the rôle of building societies it is then possible, in Chapter 4, to examine their behaviour during the 1970s, which provides the basis for this analysis. The major characteristic of the period is highly cyclical behaviour. House prices rose very rapidly, by 129 per cent, during the years 1971—73 and then fell slightly during part of 1974. The cyclical variation also extends to new mortgage advances by building societies which rose by 166 per cent between the beginning of 1970 and the summer of 1972, but fell to only 44 per cent above the 1970 level by the spring of 1974. This rapid fall was followed by a second expansion of even greater proportions, new mortgage advances being 256 per cent higher than the 1974 level by the end of 1975. In so far as figures for 1976 are available this second cycle appears to have reached its peak. Similar fluctuations occur throughout the sector. Housebuilding has for many years been a prime subject for cyclical analysis (see Gough, 1972, for example) and in the 1970s it also exhibited cyclical development. However, the rapid changes also extended to interest rates and to the flow of funds into building societies. The flow of funds for example went from record levels in the spring of 1973 to a net outflow in the first part of 1974 and back to a new record inflow in the first part of

1975. All these changes provide a striking contrast to the steady progress of the previous fifteen years. The arduous task for the main analysis is to explain not only why such major shifts took place but what the relations were between them. This analysis is presented in Chapter 5.

Up to this point the approach is largely expository, explaining the nature of the housing market in the UK, the rôle and aims of building societies as providers of housing finance and the behaviour of both sectors during the 1970s. These relationships are then formulated explicitly and their parameters estimated, after which it is possible to say that, on the basis of behaviour during the period 1955—75, a change in, say, Minimum Lending Rate, results in a change of a specified size in house prices. Chapter 6 begins by justifying the forms of the relations used and explains the parameter values obtained. Since several simultaneous relationships which are related across time are being dealt with this estimation presents considerable econometric problems. So that the text may be readily comprehensible to the non-specialist these details have been excluded from the text, but because they are of considerable importance to the specialist, the techniques which have been used and the decisions which have been made are fully explained and justified in the Technical Appendix which is fully cross-referenced with the exposition in the chapter.

In effect we have to explain the workings of three interrelated markets each with its own buyers and sellers — the housing market, the housing finance market and the building society savings market. The general structure of each of these markets can be explained quite simply. In the housing market the demand for houses by potential purchasers is largely related to their income, the price of houses, the price of alternative purchases and the cost and availability of housing finance. The supply of houses on the other hand depends on the number of existing owners who wish to sell and the level of completions of new houses by builders, plus any transfers of dwellings from other sectors, such as council housing. A large number of the house purchasers require mortgage finance from building societies, banks or other lenders to make their purchase, and the supply of these funds depends upon the liquidity position of the lenders and their own inflow of funds. Thus the supply of mortgages depends directly on the supply of funds to those bodies providing the mortgages and so there is a third market of supply and demand for funds by mortgage lenders. The simultaneous operation of these three markets not only determines the quantity of houses sold and the number and size of mortgages granted, but it also determines the price at which houses are sold, the cost of mortgages (the rate of interest) and the rate of interest offered to those wishing to lend to building societies.

Once a set of estimates is obtained, particular hypotheses concerning the behaviour of the participants during the 1970s can be considered, and this is done in Chapter 6. In particular it is possible to see how the actions of the various groups affected house prices both in the short and long run and to contrast behaviour in the 1970s with that in the 1950s and 1960s. To explain how such dramatic changes occurred in a system which previously changed only slowly, some external forces which had destabilizing effects have to be identified or it must be shown that the behaviour of some of the participants changed, either temporarily or permanently. In this way Chapter 6 establishes how building societies reacted and how this affected house prices in the 1970s.

However, the behaviour of building societies is only one of the factors affecting the level of house prices. The concluding chapter therefore considers the activities of the building societies in relation to the other forces at work during the period. In particular the rôle of the government is brought out. Its influence is very widespread, first by affecting many of the exogenous variables in the model directly, such as, Minimum Lending Rate, the standard rate of income tax, disposable incomes, local authority house sales, local authority rents, etc.; and second by influencing the mortgage interest rate both by persuasion and by a low interest loan. A further and much more difficult area to quantify is government intervention through legislation, such as the Housing Finance Acts and the establishment of 'fair rents'. These acts of legislation affect both demand and supply and thus have consequences for house prices. One action allowed for specifically in the model is the introduction of the Betterment Levy. However, this difficulty does not mean that the legislation did not have a specific effect. In particular the introduction of Competition and Credit Control in 1971 had an effect on the structure of interest rates offered by financial intermediaries. Although building societies were not primarily affected by this change they were indirectly affected in so far as major banks altered their behaviour. Since both types of institution were competing for funds, a change in the structure of interest rates affected the flow of funds into building societies.

Other factors beside the government were at work affecting the rate of increase in prices. As is common under inflation, the process of inflation feeds on itself. Both buyers' and sellers' expectations of price rises begin to increase and thus the rate of increase itself begins to increase. Furthermore these rises in price encourage people to move up the housing market into more expensive property. As prices rise the value of a mortgage on a property falls as a proportion of the value of the property and the cost of repayments (combined interest and capital) falls as a proportion of income as income rises. The house owner thus makes a capital gain which he can realize and use as a deposit on a more expensive house and take out a larger mortgage restoring the real value of repayments. This re-investment in housing of course assumes that better real rates of return are not seen to be available from other assets. Speculative moves up market will not only serve to raise prices but will also tend to maintain the new high level as owners will be unwilling to suffer real losses which may not even cover the value of the inflated mortgage which they have to pay back upon moving.

In the light of these reactions it is helpful to put forward suggestions for ways in which the rapid inflation of house prices could have been avoided. Obviously it is much easier to argue with the benefit of hindsight for actions which could not reasonably have been contemplated at the time. Nevertheless using the estimated parameters of the model the results of different courses of action can be predicted and hence preferable sequences of actions which would have avoided the excessive price rises can be suggested.

Looking backwards is only one function of Chapter 7; it is perhaps rather more interesting to consider likely developments in the housing and building society sectors in the future in the light of the experience derived from the analysis. It has been suggested that there is likely to be a second burst of inflation in house prices towards the end of the 1970s after other prices have more than made up the gap opened up at the beginning of the decade as the result of the general inflation which has been experienced. The model can be used to see if these conditions do in fact exist or are likely to occur in the near future. The experience of the early 1970s allows the signs of a coming inflation to be detected and it is thus possible to suggest some simple policy measures which will reduce the possibility of a second rapid price rise.

The scope of this book is thus considerable, despite what might seem a fairly narrow area of interest, because house prices are determined by a large number of factors, some of which act contemporaneously and others with a time lag. Hence it specifies and estimates a model not only of the housing market, but of building society behaviour as well. With this model it then traces out what occurred during the 1970s and identifies the causes of the steep rise in house prices. In particular it brings out the rôle of building societies in this inflation. Having developed such a model the book concludes by drawing the implications for policy decisions by both the building societies and the government to avoid the unwanted price rises of 1971—73 and to reduce the chance of any repetition of these events occurring again during the next few years. Hopefully the ensuing chapters are of practical value, not only in providing an analytical description of the housing market and the effects of building societies' behaviour upon it but also in suggesting a number of policy options which are available to achieve desired targets of the stable development of construction, lending, saving and prices.

2 The Structure of the UK Housing Market

This chapter explains both the nature of the housing stock in the UK over the last twenty years and the structure of the economic relations which affect the size and distribution of that stock. This will enable the identification of the rôle of house prices and the factors which determine them. Only houses which are bought and sold in the private sector of the market have an explicit price, but the sectors of the housing market are not independent. Changes in the size of say the local authority sector or the rents it charges will have repercussions for the private sector. The discussion therefore begins by considering the size and trends in the housing market as a whole before considering the behaviour of the private sector. Having established the general form of the market the relations which determine the supply and demand for private housing and the prices at which sales take place can then be developed. On this basis it will be possible to proceed to estimating the parameters of these relations given an explanation of the availability of loans for house purchase which is provided in Chapter 3.

2.1 The Development of the UK Housing Stock since 1955

The vast majority of the inhabitants of the country are housed in some identifiable unit of accommodation which can be described as a dwelling. For the sake of clarity a dwelling can be defined in the terms used in the *Census 1971 (Great Britain: County Reports, General Explanatory Notes)*: 'a structurally separate accommodation with independent access to the street or to a public staircase or hall'. It may seem rather pedantic to spell out such a careful definition, but it is common practice to talk about housing and houses as if there was some uniform asset called a house, ignoring all the distinctions which can be made between houses, flats, bungalows, maisonettes, etc. In this book the term 'house' is normally used with the meaning just shown for 'dwelling', unless the particular context explains otherwise, thus following what is normal practice in not only common parlance but the housing literature as well.

During the twenty years 1951—71 the stock of dwellings enumerated in the Census in Great Britain rose from 13.3 million to 18.9 million representing a rate of growth of some 1.7 per cent in the 1950s and 1.5 per cent in the 1960s. Figure 2.1 (c) shows that during the last decade this rise in the total stock has been fairly steady, fluctuating largely between 1 and 2 per cent per year. This does not mean that the construction of new dwellings has proceeded smoothly, because the vast discrepancy in size between the number of new dwellings completed and the size of the existing stock entails that a small fluctuation in the stock represents a very large fluctuation in completions. In 1968, the year when completions were at a maximum, they only formed 2.3 per cent of the existing stock, and by 1974 a further 1 per cent change in the stock would have entailed a 71 per cent change in the number of completions. It is worth noting at the outset therefore that even small changes in the demand for the stock of housing would represent very large changes in the demand for new housing — assuming of course that the lack of homogeneity between new and existing housing in terms of age, location, size, facilities and condition can largely be set aside.

Figure 2.1 (a) shows that completions have fluctuated very widely during the last twenty years. These fluctuations are part of a cyclical pattern. Between 1956 and 1963 completions varied round an average of 300,000 a year with a minimum point of 278,633 in 1958. From 1963 onwards there is a rapid expansion up to a peak of 425,835 completions in 1968, but since that date completions have fallen more rapidly to a new low of 278,363 dwellings in 1974, lower even that that achieved in 1958. This cycle would have been even clearer had it not been for the very severe winter of 1963 when completions were only about 65 per cent of what would have been expected from the trend through the surrounding periods. There is some evidence that the cycle has passed its nadir and that completions in 1975 and 1976 represent a slight up-turn, although it is rather too soon to comment on the likely future direction of change.

The stock will also be affected by the conversion of existing dwellings into larger or smaller numbers of units and by closures and demoli-

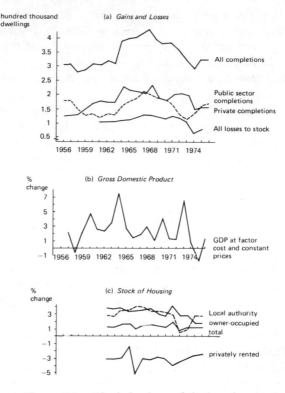

Figure 2.1   The behaviour of the housing stock

tions, but these numbers are rather smaller. In 1972, for example, 319,000 new dwellings were constructed while only 10,000 dwellings were added by other means. Losses on the other hand amounted to 89,000 dwellings due to slum clearance and 27,000 for other reasons, a total of 116,000 losses. Thus the total increase in the stock in 1972 was the difference between 329,000 gains and 116,000 losses, i.e. approximately 213,000 dwellings. In percentage terms losses are 35 per cent of gains, and the gains, losses and net increase represent 1.7, 0.6 and 1.1 per cent respectively of the pre-existing stock. The number of losses per year unlike the number of completions remained fairly steady during the period, with, as is shown in Figure 2.1 (a), a small rise and then a larger fall in 1974, roughly coincident with the pattern of completions. Losses are in fact much more closely related to completions in the public sector alone with a lead of one or two years because the majority of the losses are due to slum clearance and rebuilding schemes.

Before considering why the stock has changed in the way it has and what influences the level of new completions, the three main categories of tenure of housing must be distinguished. These are owner-occupation, renting from a public authority (usually a local authority or new town corporation), and renting from a private landlord. Other arrangements such as housing associations do exist but form a very small part of the total; however, when considering subjects such as security of tenure, a further useful distinction can be made between renting furnished and unfurnished properties in the private sector. Concentrating on the original three sectors for the time being, the housing stock in 1960 was divided between them in the proportions 42 per cent for the owner-occupied sector, 27 per cent for renting from a public authority and 32 per cent for renting privately. By the end of 1975, however, the picture had changed radically and the share of the owner-occupied sector had risen to 53 per cent, so that the majority of people owned their homes. The public sector also had an increased share at 31 per cent, although this does not represent such a large change. To permit this increase in shares, the proportion rented in the private sector has consequently fallen to only 16 per cent. The pattern of this change can be seen in Figure 2.1 (c). The reduction in the privately rented sector represents not only a fall in share but a fall in the absolute number of dwellings as well by some 37 per cent between 1960 and 1974. The number of privately rented dwellings fell in every quarter over that period while the stocks of owner-occupied and publicly rented dwellings increased monotonically. Local authority house sales thus never outstripped the new construction of public sector housing although the net increase in 1972 and 1973 was small after closures and demolitions are also subtracted. While the overall stock of housing rose by 21 per cent between 1960 and 1974 the owner-occupied sector increased by 51 per cent and the publicly rented sector by 42 per cent.

It is important to note in discussing the aggregate distribution of the stock of housing by tenure that this distribution is not consistent across the entire country. In particular in Scotland and Northern Ireland the owner-occupied sector has had a much smaller share of the total stock. However, this does not contradict the general proposition that there has been a trend towards owner-occupation throughout the country over the last two decades. It is also true that the trend towards renting from the public sector and the reduction of private renting has been generally observed although of course the actual values of the percentage change in each area are not necessarily the same.

In Figure 2.1 the components of the changes in the stock have not all exhibited the same time path as their sum, which is not surprising in view of the different economic determinants of the various sectors. Taking Figure 2.1 (a) first, completions in the private sector have followed a less smooth path than completions in the public sector. The growth up to an initial maximum in 1964 was rather steeper than for the public sector, but while total completions continued to rise up till 1968 private sector completions fell successively in 1965, 1966 and 1967. Public sector completions in those years thus more than compensated for the fall in private sector completions. During 1971 to 1973 the opposite picture is observed, while private sector completions rose public sector completions fell sufficiently steeply that there was a fall in total. At the end of the period the initial experience is repeated with public sector completions keeping to higher levels than private sector completions and hence total completions recover from their very low value in 1974.

The relative movements in public and private sector completions are more clearly understood by comparing them with the movements in the overall level of activity as indicated by the percentage change in GDP in Figure 2.1 (b). With the exception of 1970 completions in the private sector tend to follow the path of GDP. The peaks in 1960, 1964, 1968 and 1973 are all matched. However, the peaks in the private housing sector are real peaks in the sense that output is actually lower on both sides of the peak whereas with the minor exception of 1958 and the more major exception of 1975 the cycles in real GDP are only cycles in the rate of growth, output does not actually fall after the peak it merely rises more slowly. The housebuilding cycles are thus stronger than the general economic cycles. Public sector completions on the other hand follow a somewhat different course. Although they fall with the trough in GDP in 1958 there is no recovery until 1964 after which they continue to rise in 1967. The new surge in private completions in 1971 to 1973 is completely missed with completions in the public sector falling even faster from their 1967 maximum. On the other hand the minimum for the whole period is attained in 1973 rather than 1974 for the private sector and completions continue to rise into 1976. To some extent this pattern is counter-cyclical although not totally so. The public sector cycles have a greater amplitude and period than the private sector ones. There are only two cycles for the public sector as opposed to four for the private sector.

To some extent these different cycles reflect the different economic determinants of the two sectors. The private sector moves clearly in line with the general economic cycle whereas the public sector reflects government policy which to some extent seeks to counter the cyclical behaviour of the economy as a whole. Hadjimatheou (1976) gives a very clear summary of the reasons which have been put forward for the pro-cyclical behaviour of the private sector. This behaviour is the more interesting because of its contrast with that observed in the US where investment in private housing is counter-cyclical. There the argument, as summarized in Evans (1969), runs that the returns to investment in housing are relatively low compared to investment in other industries, hence in times of expansion labour will be bid away from the residential construction industry (mainly into industrial construction) and so output of houses will be held back. In times of depression on the other hand although wages for residential construction may be relatively low employment tends to be preferable to unemployment and output can pick up. A second argument made by Alberts (1962) and Guttentag (1961), following the same rationale, is that funds for mortgages are bid away from the housing market during the upturn by relatively attractive interest rates, the converse being true in the downturn. Not surprisingly the argument for the UK experience is rather different and can best be explained by suggesting what it is that affects the demand and supply of housing.

2.2   The Demand for Housing

Although housing, like most other products, has a demand largely dependent upon the number of possible purchasers, their financial ability to purchase, its price and the price of competing products it is difficult to obtain a clear specification of the exact form of the relation. Our interest here is in the private sector and the public sector is only relevant in so far as it affects demand in the private sector. However, even within the private sector one can purchase housing in two senses, either by buying the building or by purchasing the housing services available from it. If demand is considered in terms of the flow of housing services then it is possible to deal with owner-occupiers and those renting property in a similar fashion, because owner-occupiers can be treated as paying an imputed rent to themselves for living in their homes in the same way as is done in the National Accounts (see *National Income and Expenditure, 1966—76,* for example). The attraction of considering the demand for housing services rather than for the property itself is that only a small proportion of the housing stock is being bought or sold during either a year or a quarter, and with the rapid rise in prices which we are seeking to explain frequent observations are needed. However, the consumption of housing services is only one reason why people seek to own their homes; a second reason is as an asset with a yield. House prices have risen every year since the war, so owning a house is a means of protecting one's wealth from the inroads of general inflation.

There is no straightforward means of incorporating these two sources of demand, first because of the discontinuties in the housing market and second because of the availability of data. Although we are interested in private house prices, it is ironically easiest to begin with the public sector. The demand for public authority hosuing very clearly outstrips the supply in most areas of the country as is evidenced by the length of waiting lists. Local authority housing is not allocated by any market mechanism but by an assessment of the relative need of the prospective tenant by the local authority usually according to some system of points which takes into account such factors as family circumstances, current accommodation and the length of time the applicant has been waiting. Rents are subsidized for all tenants out of local and national taxation and rents are subsidized specifically for individual tenants on the basis of their ability to pay through a system of rebates. The public sector is clearly not in equilibrium, supply determines the number of households housed, and the price (rent) is administered.

The public sector can thus be taken as an exogenous factor rather than a section of the housing market in general whose parameters have to be solved simultaneously with those of the private sector. This conceals some small difficulties owing to regional imbalance. Not all public authorities face excess demand, particularly some New Town Corporations. Also the fact of a tenancy in one authority does not give the right of transfer to another area nor does the position on the housing waiting list of one authority enable a transfer to a similar place on another authority's list. Thus what is true in aggregate may have some regional exceptions where a real choice exists in any one time period between the public and private sectors; but this problem is unlikely to cause much distortion. The inability to transfer on the other hand strengthens the separability of the public and private sectors and gives considerable rigidity to the mobility of households in the UK.

It is thus justifiable to treat the private sector separately as is normal in models of the housing market. (See Whitehead (1974) or Hadjimatheou (1976) for surveys of the literature relating to the UK and Ricks (1973) for recent work in the US.) The private sector itself is comprised of a number of different categories of tenure which affect the assessment of demand. The largest sector is those who are owner-occupiers, followed by those who rent from a private landlord. However, there are also dwellings which form second homes and those which are in multiple occupancy, either with more than one household renting a single dwelling or with the owner sharing a dwelling with a tenant. All these factors lead to difficulties. Clearly there is some relation between renting and owner-occupation. Provided the property is suitable a landlord would wish to sell if the return from renting fell too far compared with the price of the property; but this assumes transfers between sectors are readily possible. Security of tenure through the Rent Acts on un-furnished properties, and since 1974 on some furnished properties as well, means that transfer is not always possible. If the property is sold its value will depend quite substantially on whether or not there is vacant possession. Furthermore controls on rents themselves affect the attractiveness and marketability of rented properties. There are thus important restrictions in the market for existing property in the private sector (other than for short-run occupation). Cooper and Stafford (1975) show that the system of 'fair rents' introduced in 1965, leads to rents below the market level because the fair rent is that which would prevail were supply and demand in long-run equilibrium, rather than that which actually prevails with current excess demand — excess demand which is ironically aided by the restrictions on the system themselves which discourage the provision of rented accommodation by landlords.

To a large extent the problem of the division in the private sector is removed if new housing is considered rather than the stock of housing as a whole. When housing is new, apart from some constraints on parti-cular sorts of multi-dwelling buildings, the difficulties imposed by security of tenure and the control of rents do not affect the initial purchase price or the allocation between owner-occupation and private renting. This is particularly fortunate because the quarterly construc-tion statistics which are available (in *Economic Trends* and the *Monthly Digest*) do not distinguish between these two forms of tenure. This sort of pragmatic approach, while absolutely necessary in order to achieve a model which can actually be estimated is rather unattractive from the point of view of economic rationale. What would be preferable is a soundly based economic specification which leads to a model which can be estimated.

It was stated initially that the general form of the demand equation was that housing was a function of the financial ability to buy, the number of possible purchasers, price and the price of competing products. There are two ways in which such a specification can be achieved, either by expressing a direct flow demand for housing, i.e. the demand for the net change in the quantity of housing, or by obtaining an adjustment model of the demand for the stock of housing. The choice here has been to express this as a demand for the change in the stock of housing, allowing for the fact that the stock of housing does not adjust completely to its desired level in each time period.

On the whole people move house at long and irregular intervals (once every 7—10 years on the basis of mortgage and census data); the costs of moving are considerable, both in financial terms at around £1,000 for the average transaction and in terms of adjusting to new circumstances such as schooling if the move is anything more than a short distance. People, therefore, do not tend to move as a matter of a slight whim, but to make a major step such as changing employment or making a substantial shift in type (and probably price) of house. Other sales occur on a much more stable basis because of the death of the owner, but in general this means that changes in the overall demand for housing will be relatively slow to have effect. In any case new houses are not sold because of the death of the previous owner! Thus although new housing represents only one or at most two per cent of the total stock of housing and would be subject to dramatic changes in demand if the demand for the stock changed substantially, the costs of change are sufficiently high that most short-run factors have an insignificant effect on demand. Many of the changes due to changes in family composition (death and marriage) will compensate each other giving only small aggregate effects. It should therefore be possible to estimate relatively stable flow models under the normal circumstances which prevailed during the 1950s and 1960s.

The stock of housing in the private sector changes in each time period as the net result of additions in the form of completions of new houses and transfers from the public sector through sales of local authority housing, and substractions from closures and demolitions for slum clearance or other reasons. Whitehead (1974) in her model of the housing market neglects the effects of transfers from the public sector and reductions in the existing stock, arguing quite correctly that no accurate figures on a quarterly basis are available for closures and demolitions; however, such an omission must have a cost of some degree of importance. As discussed in Section 2.1 closures are related to completions in the public sector and local authority house sales are not always negligible.

Leaving out local authority house sales is a sensible step as local authority house sales are normally to sitting tenants who have little reason to move into the owner-occupied sector by buying a different house. In any case the price agreed for sales to a sitting tenant is usually only a fraction of the open market price to take the previous payment of rents into account. Hence there is little substitutability between the tenant's house and other houses and local authority house sales can be dropped from the analysis.

The problem here is thus to decide how to treat closures and demolitions. The practical reason for omitting it from the analysis is that it is not measured with great accuracy, but it would be more reassuring to have an economic justification as well. The residual change in the stock represents a number of different factors, the most important of which is the closure or demolition of property because it is no longer fit for habitation. A second cause of premature closure or demolition is for redevelopment, leaving a residual which is largely composed of changes due to conversions which are not included in the statistics of new constructions. These last changes may either decrease or increase the stock as several new flats can be obtained from a single large existing house and several small cottages can be knocked together to form larger dwellings.

The three components of net closures and demolitions outlined can be incorporated in a simple indirect manner. Taking closures because houses are no longer fit for habitation first: since housing is being treated as an asset these closures are equivalent to a form of depreciation. A crude measure of depreciation would therefore be a simple function of the stock which could depreciate. Moving on to the second cause, premature closure or demolition for redevelopment, most of these closures will be related to new housing started either in the same time period or in the reasonably near future. Lastly, net closures due to conversions will be fairly closely related to current completions. In general the higher the level of completions the greater the number of conversions reflecting the higher level of building activity. In fact it may well be that if there is demand pressure for new housing this can be relieved partly by the conversion of existing properties although as already noted some conversions can reduce the stock of dwellings instead of increasing it. Assuming that all losses to the stock have been accounted for closures and demolitions can now be incorporated into an estimatable model.

This provides justification for estimating a demand function for housing in the private sector which is both economically meaningful and practicable where completions of new private houses are determined by the financial ability to buy, the number of potential purchasers, prices, the prices of competing products and the size of the existing stock of private houses. In fact this leads to framing the whole of the analysis in terms of the market for new private houses. As is discussed in Chapter 4, the information available on house prices relates to the price of new houses and this chapter also looks at the relationship between building society lending and these prices.

Before leaving this section, some consideration should be given to the specification of financial ability and the numbers of possible purchasers, both of which are somewhat nebulous variables at present and also to the incorporation of the asset-holding function of housing. Taking financial ability first, in considering the demand for new houses, we are looking at the net change in asset holding, allowing for partial adjustment, not the overall holding of assets, we therefore need to be able to incorporate people's ability to accumulate new wealth, and this will be determined by income and the ability and willingness to borrow. Borrowing in this case will be largely from building societies, because as is noted in Chapter 4 they provide the large majority of loans for house purchase at the rate of interest which they set. Income will be defined to exclude short-run or transitory fluctuations following the discussion on p. 16. Thus we can decompose financial ability to buy into a measure of income which excludes short-run fluctuations, new mortgage advances by building societies, mortgage lending by other institutions and the rate of interest on mortgage borrowing.

The number of people who form the basis of the demand is rather more difficult to deal with. It is not really the entire population because although some form of housing is a necessity and hence every one has some sort of 'need' to be housed, people are normally housed in groups as well as individuals, where most of the groupings will be on a family basis. These groups (and individuals) can be described, in a somewhat tautological way, as households where these are individuals living on their own or groups who eat together and have a common expenditure. There is no one to one correspondence between dwellings and households, because a dwelling may be occupied by more than one household or a household may have more than one dwelling, a second home. Further, the number of households currently in existence is affected by the number and price of dwellings. Children may not wish to live with their parents, but may be constrained to do so through lack of alternative accommodation. It is therefore necessary to choose the specification of the demand as a function of the population very carefully.

Our concern is with the number of households which would have been formed in the past in the absence of housing and other constraints. If the constraints are varied then the demand for housing can change considerably over a short period and this must be incorporated into any model of demand. In his comments on a draft of this book Mark Boléat, Under-Secretary of the Building Societies Association, stressed the importance of the existence of this body of underlying demand from potential householders who would like to own a house were it not for the constraints on entering the market at all. In so far as there is any distinction between the determinants of demand by potential first-time buyers and existing owners, complications are introduced into the explanation and the determination of the number of potential households is very important.

The problem of the determination of the number of potential households is particularly important in trying to make forecasts of housing demand and the Green Paper on Housing Policy (Cmnd 6851, 1977) devotes a large section of its Technical Volume (pt I, pp. 110– 163) just to the discussion of this. Potential households or 'underlying demand' are just as difficult to estimate for the present or past as the future since we can only obtain indicators of their size and not measure them directly. The number of marriages, of course, is an indicator of potential new households as deaths is an indicator of the reduction in the number of households, but there is considerable difficulty to using them accurately. Marriages have striking seasonal patterns to quite some extent related to the tax provisions. In the 1960s, for example, the married person's allowance was given for the whole year irrelevant of the date of marriage within it so there was a peak of marriages just before the end of the tax year in early April. In the first part of the 1970s the bride received a full single person's allowance both as a single person and then in her married state thus encouraging marriages towards the middle of the tax year. Other indicators of the number of potential households are available from sources such as local authority waiting lists, but they also have major drawbacks. First, those who put their names on local authority lists are not likely to be potential house purchasers in the immediate future. Second, the length of lists is governed by both supply and demand factors in the market for local authority housing; and third, potential households for house purchase may not be formed at rates which bear any relation to the rates of formation of potential local authority tenants. Therefore despite the attractiveness of determining potential households as shown by Holmans (1970) it is unlikely that much use can be made of any variable except population as a whole and perhaps some sort of trend to take account of social change. The nature of this trend is very clearly set out in Part II of the Technical Volume from the Green Paper on Housing Policy (Cmnd 6851, 1977).

Finally, in order to allow for the asset demand for housing as well as the demand for housing as a necessity and a luxury service some measure of the rate of return must be incorporated. In one sense the rate of return which can be achieved is the implicit value of the rent which could be derived from the property were it rented. It is worthwhile for house owners to hold their property as an asset provided that the rate of return on the property is greater than the rate of interest payable on borrowing money to buy it. To assess this asset against others, then one must compare the rate of return with other possible rates of return, taking account of the fact that the rate of interest on mortgage borrowing is not normally the same as the rate of interest on borrowing for other purposes. Using the mortgage rate alone for the cost of holding a house is rather too simplistic as it assumes that mortgage finance is used for the entire purchase. In so far as other funds are used a general rate of interest available for long-term lending by persons is the correct variable, say the long-term local authority rate. Thus the true cost would be a weighted average where the average ratio of mortgage advances to the value of house sales gives the appropriate weights. The FRB—MIT—Penn model (reported in Kalchbrenner, 1973) actually incorporates this in its housing section, but does this with a rather different supply function from that suggested in Section 2.3, so their method cannot be used here directly. In any case it is arguable that it is the marginal not the average cost of borrowing which is the effective rate of interest for the decision-making and that it is the deposit (for mortgages of less than 100 per cent) which imposes the constraint rather than the mortgage rate of interest. The relative attractiveness of housing compared to other products will be shown by relative price but the choice of other products is difficult to specify. Whitehead (1974) argues on the basis of the available evidence that since existing housing is such a close substitute the prices of new and existing housing will move together anyway and since imperfections prevent easy transfers to other tenures, the appropriate price is consumer products in general and not investment goods as the real choice facing the ordinary home owner is between raising a mortgage for house purchase or not borrowing. It is possible to test whether there may be an implicit relation between house price, the cost of finance and the imputable rent in equilibrium by including the general rate of interest on long-run lending by persons among the arguments of the demand function. This will be sufficient to take account of both investment and service demands for housing although, if house purchase is an explicit hedge against inflation, price expectations must also be included.

Summarizing the conclusions about the form of financial ability to purchase, the number of potential buyers and price, the final general specification of the demand for housing is:

$$\mathrm{HCP}_t = f_1\,(\mathrm{Y, MA, MO, IM, NP,}\ t,\ \mathrm{PH, PC, ILAL, PHE,}$$

$$\mathrm{PCE,\ HP}_{t-1}) \tag{1}$$

where,

HCP   is private house completions (all variables are defined in full with sources and units of measurement in the Technical Appendix, pp. 131–3)

Y   is personal disposable income excluding short-run fluctuations

MA   is new mortgage advances by building societies

MO   is new lending by other institutions on mortgage

IM   is the building society rate of interest on mortgage lending

NP   is the population of Great Britain

t is a time trend

PH   is the average price of new houses

PC   is the consumer price index

ILAL is the local authority loan rate of interest

PHE   and PCE   are the expectations of PH and PC

and   HP   is the stock of private housing.

This specification will require some adjustment in detail for the purposes of estimation and this is considered in Chapter 5, but in the meantime the supply of housing can be discussed.

2.3   The Supply of Housing

In looking at the behaviour of the number of completions of new private housing the main feature of note was its wide cyclical fluctuations. The demand function which has just been analysed reflects some of these cyclical factors by variables such as personal disposable income, mortgage lending, interest rates and prices which fluctuate themselves either in absolute terms in the case of interest rates or round a rising trend for the other variables. These fluctuations alone are not sufficient to explain the full cycle in housebuilding, supply also has a rôle to play.

Since the completion of a house requires as a necessary condition that construction of the house be started previously, and hence the number of completions could be closely related to the number of starts with a distributed lag. If this relation is purely technological then it says nothing about the economic determinants of the supply of housing, it merely means that starts have to be explained, instead of completions. The pattern of supply which would be observed in response to a change in demand is that in the short-run demand can only be met by completing houses which are under construction. In the longer run the number of starts can also be increased so that there is a larger number of houses to complete. Thus there would be both a shortening in the average period of construction and an increase in both starts and completions. The lags in the system will affect the number of houses under construction, if starts cannot match completions then the number of houses under construction will fall despite the increase in demand, or if demand falls before houses started are completed then completions will fall and hence the number of houses under construction will rise.

Figure 2.2 shows how these three variables have moved. The most obvious characteristic is that as construction rose between 1956 and 1964 starts exceeded completions and the number of houses under construction at the end of each year was lower than either of these. While output remained at its peak between 1964 and 1968 the three series moved together, but when the market turned down after 1968 the number of houses under construction rose, both above starts and

Houses started, under construction and completed

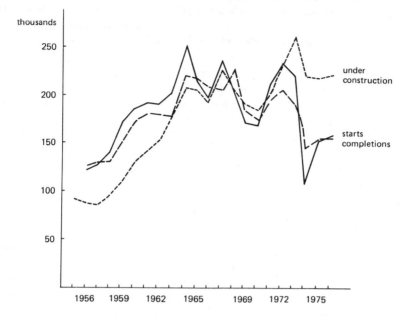

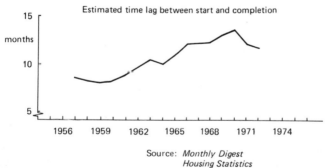

Estimated time lag between start and completion

Source: *Monthly Digest*
Housing Statistics
Housing and Construction Statistics

Figure 2.2   The construction of houses for private owners

completions and in absolute terms. This reflects two factors, first that many houses remained incomplete often because their builders had gone into liquidation, and second that in 1970 to 1973 completions did not respond strongly to the new boom in starts in the way that the 1967 increase in starts was followed by the 1968 increase in completions. Starts on the whole are more volatile than completions, showing that if houses become difficult to sell, builders react more by not starting new work than by not completing existing work, and that if demand rises this is reflected rather more by an increase in starts than an increase in completions, which may not feed through the system while the demand is still higher. This latter is clear from the time lag between starts and completions shown in the lower graph of Figure 2.2. During the period graphed it took between three and four quarters on average to complete a house. Ignoring the temporary peak caused by the bad winter of 1963 the major increases in the construction time lag took place during 1965 to 1970 when the main period of growth in housebuilding had come to an end. The increased lag is, therefore, more likely to be due to deliberate actions on the part of builders rather than high levels of construction entailing the use of more difficult sites and hence delays for technological reasons.

Despite the existence of the construction lag completions tended to show turning points in the same year as starts with the exception of 1967—68. This suggests that both are influenced by economic factors simultaneously and that the suggested distributed lag is not a purely technological relation. This is reflected in estimates of the lag where if a lag distributed over 0 to 7 quarters is taken the following weights are obtained:

lag:	0	1	2	3	4	5	6	8
coefficient:	0.33	0.13	0.12	0.04	0.00	0.04	0.07	0.08

with an average lag of only 6.5 months. The shape of lag distribution is also not what would be expected from a technological relation which would give the largest weights to lags of 2, 3 and 4 quarters, the weights dropping rapidly away thereafter. The distribution quoted above is the same form as those found by Hadjimatheou (1976) and Whitehead (1974) with different data periods and lengths of distribution. Attempts to impose the technological shape are not successful and the quoted distribution is very robust to different estimation techniques (see Technical Appendix, pp. 137—8). Extending the time lag distribution to include more previous periods did not improve the explanation.

Given this robustness there is support for the suggestion that the appropriate supply function to estimate is one for starts, using the distributed lag to link starts and completions. A straightforward specification of such a supply function would suggest that output was a function of the relative cost of inputs to output, given, in view of the lag between the start of construction and the payment on sale, the cost and availability of finance to housebuilders. Due allowance must also be made for the fluctuations due to the season of the year. In practice there are some drawbacks to this precise specification as costs are only available with a measure of profit already included. It is also not possible to get a direct estimate of the availability of finance, therefore in estimating in Chapter 5 new lending for house purchase is used as a measure of the general attitude towards the financing of housing. This is not a perfect estimator but it seems to act as a useful proxy. Other variables relating to the general availability of credit and the money supply proved less satisfactory.

The major alternative specification is to adopt the approach of say the Treasury model (HM Treasury, 1977) and estimate investment expenditures on housing rather than starts. (Hadjimatheou (1976) also has this as an extra equation.) It is then presumably possible to relate this either to completions or starts by some appropriate weighting although numbers of dwellings and the level of investment may behave differently if there are changes in the distribution of the types of houses being built. However, unlike the macro-models of the economy we have no interest in investment expenditures as such so this variable can be omitted. In any case we would be using exactly the opposite rationale to the London Business School model (London Graduate School of Business Studies, 1976) who estimate a starts equation and then derive investment expenditure on private housing from lagged starts. We shall therefore stick to the specification outlined.

2.4   The Determination of House Prices

It now remains to resolve the interaction of supply and demand through the determination of prices. The main endogenous variables in the private sector of the housing market to explain are: the price of new housing, the number of new houses completed and the number of new houses started (setting the stock of private sector housing on one side as that is determined by an identity which can be estimated recursively). There are three equations to explain these three unknowns. (This system can therefore be solved as it clearly meets the rank condition for identification, and a brief examination of the equations shows that the order condition is also met.) The specified structure does not, however, yield a direct estimate of the price of new housing, the very variable which is uppermost in our interests. There is no problem in principle with this as the simultaneous solution of the structure will yield an estimate for PH. Nevertheless this can be approached more directly by specifying equation (1) in the form of a price equation rather than a quantity equation. In doing this there is no departure from previous experience as the London Business School model, the Treasury model, and Neuberger and Nichol (1976) all use price equations. The main rationale for having a price function is, however, based on economic reasoning. As already seen completions are closely determined by starts, with in practice some short-run response to changes in interest rates and house prices. Price, therefore, is largely determined by the movements in demand given the largely predetermined level of the number of new houses available. In fact according to Neuberger and Nichol completions only depend directly on past prices.

This, therefore, completes the explanation of the housing market as it affects this analysis. The major point to note here is the important rôle played by finance in both supply and demand. It is this which shows the link between the building societies and house prices. Since we are seeking to explain building societies' behaviour and hence their pattern of lending our housing market equation will form part of a larger simultaneous equation system which includes a building societies' model. This is developed in Chapter 3.

3 The Rôle of Building Societies

3.1 Introduction

The purchase and sale of their homes are usually the largest and most important transactions undertaken by people. Houses normally cost several times the purchasers' gross annual income and hence it takes many years to be able to accumulate sufficient wealth to be able to purchase a house outright. The majority of houses are therefore purchased with the aid of borrowed funds, and building societies provide the large majority of these funds (over 75 per cent in 1975). It is thus very clear that building societies have a crucial rôle to play in the purchase of housing, and that changes in their lending behaviour are likely to have direct effects on the demand for housing.

Like any other financial intermediary building societies are not only lenders but also borrowers. Traditionally they borrow most of their funds from small savers, many of whom hope that the fact of their lending to a society will in itself make it more likely that they will be able to obtain a mortgage from the same society. However, other factors such as security, the attractive rates of interest compared to alternative possibilities such as deposit accounts with banks, savings banks and Post Office accounts, and the ease of withdrawal mean that over half the small savings by persons are currently held by building societies. (Revell (1973b), table 5, estimates that in 1970 the percentage was 51.1.) Building societies therefore also play a very important rôle as a savings institution for persons in the UK.

In order to consider the lending behaviour of building societies fully their behaviour as borrowers and competitors in the market for funds with other financial institutions must also be examined.

27

3.2   The Structure of Building Societies

In 1975 there were 382 building societies in the UK, but almost all of these (93 per cent in 1971) were small with total assets of under £10 million, representing together less than 5 per cent of the total assets of the building society movement. The largest five societies alone had over 50 per cent of the assets in 1971. So from a practical point of view the behaviour of the mortgage market as a whole is substantially determined by the activities of about twenty societies. This concentration of assets is part of a continuing trend. Between 1960 and 1975 the number of societies has fallen by nearly 50 per cent, most of the reduction occurring among the very small societies which have been absorbed by larger ones.

Building societies are very specialized financial intermediaries, operating almost exclusively in the markets for personal savings and in loans for house purchase to persons. They are not profit-making institutions in the normal sense and are mutual organizations or friendly societies many of which are governed by borrowers as well as savers. The purpose of their existence is to provide housing loans and to provide a rate of return for their investors. The provision of housing loans is the dominant feature, but they would not have any funds to lend if they did not offer an attractive rate of interest to savers. As is clear from Table 3.1 the large majority of their assets is in the form of mortgages secured on owner-occupied residential property and related insurance policies. The remaining assets other than a small amount of their own property for their offices and local branches are in the form of liquid assets. The general structure of the assets and liabilities is shown in Table 3.2. The end-of-year book values of these assets in 1975

Table 3.1. Structure of building societies

	£million		
	1955	1965	1975
Total assets	2,075	5,594	24,364
Mortgages outstanding	1,761	4,583	18,882
Shares and deposits	1,959	5,159	22,696
New mortgages advanced (net)	179	459	2,768
Increase in shares and deposits	187	651	4,172

Source: Financial Statistics

Table 3.2. Balance sheet of building societies

Assets		% in 1975	Liabilities		% in 1975
Mortgage assets	(AM)	77.5	Shares and deposits	(SD)	93.2
Liquid assets	(AL)	21.1	Reserves	(R)	3.3
Other assets (land,			Accrued interest	(AI)	1.1
buildings etc.)	(AO)	1.4	Official loans	(GL)	0.1
			Other liabilities	(OL)	2.3
Total assets	(ATOT)	100.0	Total liabilities	(LTOT)	100.0

Source: Financial Statistics

were comprised of: cash and balances with banks 2.6 per cent; sterling certificates of deposit 1.1 per cent; Treasury bills 0.2 per cent; local authority temporary debt 2.7 per cent; local authority long-term debt 5.7 per cent; British government securities (a) up to 5 years 7.2 per cent, (b) 5—15 years 1.5 per cent, (c) over 15 years 0.1 per cent; land building and equipment 1.3 per cent; other assets 0.1 per cent; compared with mortgages which formed 77.5 per cent. The liquid assets have to form at least 7.5 per cent of each society's total assets otherwise a society is liable to lose its Trustee Status and membership of the Building Societies Association and a maximum maturity period of five years is applied to this minimum 7.5 per cent. Liquid assets held in excess of 7.5 per cent are not subject to this maturity constraint. Obviously the aggregate figures given for 1975 do not reflect the portfolios of each individual society, but since the picture is dominated by the few major societies it is a clear indicator of how they choose to behave. In particular note that the liquidity ratio implicit in these figures is 21.1 per cent greatly in excess of the required 7.5 per cent, and we shall return to this discrepancy shortly.

The liabilities of the societies are primarily in the form of deposits by small savers. These deposits are held in a number of forms: some are held as deposits for a fixed time period, usually one to three years; others are in the form of a contract to subscribe regular amounts at one- or three-monthly intervals; thirdly some are held as part of the Save-As-You-Earn scheme; and, most commonly, amounts are held in an account where deposits can be made at any time and withdrawals, while nominally at seven days notice, can be made on demand, although there are limitations of, for example, £50 in cash or £1,000 in the form of a cheque which vary between societies. These latter amounts and the regular subscription accounts usually involve the nominal purchase of shares in the society. The regular subscription accounts normally have quite low maximum limits of around £32 per month and the ordinary share accounts a limitation of £15,000 per individual. Of course there is nothing to stop anyone investing several lots of £15,000 with a number of different societies. The large majority of accounts contain only small sums of money; in 1975 the total value of shares and deposits was £22,696 million held in 18 million accounts, and thus the average balance was approximately £1,250. The remaining liabilities consisted of: accrued interest 1.1 per cent; official loans 0.1 per cent; reserves 3.3 per cent; and other liabilities 2.3 per cent. It is clear from these data that the required reserve ratio is small. In fact it varies inversely with the size of the total assets of the individual society. A ratio of 2.5 per cent is required for the first £100 million of assets, 2 per cent for the assets between £100 million and £500 million, 1.5 per cent between £500 million and £1,000 million and 1.25 per cent for all assets thereafter. Hence as the size and concentration of societies continues over time one would expect to observe the steady dimunation in the overall ratio which has occurred, from 4.62 per cent in 1955 to the 3.3 per cent shown for 1975.

The degree of formal external control exercised over the building societies is small — the liquidity and reserve ratios are, for example, required by the Building Societies Association, an organization to which most societies including all the major ones belong as well as being a required condition for Trustee Status. The Council of the Building Societies Association, which is drawn from the member societies, also makes recommendations about the level and structure of interest rates in the light of the overall financial position of the building society movement. The individual societies are not compelled to follow these recommendations, but not surprisingly most societies, including the larger ones, do. The main legal controls on building societies have been incorporated in various specific pieces of legislation, although most of the important points were drawn together in the Building Societies Act of 1962. The Chief Registrar of Friendly Societies lays down a number of limits on such subjects as advertising and the composition of investments. The main control on the societies outside the formal framework comes in the form of government pressure. Considerable influence has been brought to bear on various occasions during the

1970s, either to defer increase in the mortgage rates or to reduce the rate. In 1974, for example, the societies were given a £500 million government loan to help them peg interest rates. Again in 1976 interest rates were lowered reluctantly from 11 to 10.5 per cent in April in response to government pressure only to be raised rapidly by a record margin to 12.25 per cent in October.

The structure to be explained is therefore quite complex. However, it is a simple matter to set out the main variables representing the building societies' activities. First, the balance sheet from Table 3.1 and the information given above can be itemized as is shown in Table 3.2 with the names of the variables in parentheses. Second the level of the two sets of interest rates which building societies fix (the mortgage rates and the savings rates) must be determined.

As Table 3.2 is a balance sheet ATOT $\equiv$ LTOT, and OL is the residual balancing item:

$$OL \equiv AM + AL + AO - (SD + R + AI + GL) . \qquad (1)$$

Only seven independent quantities have been defined in the ten variables mentioned. The liquidity and reserve ratios can also be defined in terms of these variables as LR $\equiv$ AL/ATOT and RR $\equiv$ R/LTOT $\equiv$ R/ATOT without creating any further independent variables. Any explanation of building society behaviour must therefore be sufficient to explain these twelve variables uniquely by determining their seven independent components.

The choice of the order of formulation of the accounting identities and the choice of the seven independent factors to explain depends upon the interpretation made of what it is that building societies are actually trying to do. Accounting conventions themselves tell us relatively little; we must look to economic analysis.

If building societies operated very closely either to fixed or to the minimum required liquidity and reserve ratios it would be possible to estimate most of the variables simply by determining any one of total assets, mortgages outstanding, liquid assets, reserves or the stock of shares and deposits subject of course to the aggregation problem affecting the reserve and liquidity ratios which we have mentioned already. For example, if we could determine the stock of shares and deposits (SD), the amount available as a basis for relending as mortgage advances is determined by the liquidity ratio as SD(1 − LR). Lending could then be determined on the basis of the reserve ratio as a simple multiple of the original deposit:

$$AM = \frac{1}{(1 - RR)} SD(1 - LR), \tag{2}$$

as with other financial institutions. However, societies operate with fluctuating liquidity ratios which are well within the required limits, so a wider explanation is required. Before continuing the aims of building society behaviour must be established and a suitable model to estimate the relations derived must be constructed.

3.3   The Aims of Building Societies

It is always difficult to decide in economics what it is that people are trying to do because the evidence available tends to be either incomplete or conflicting. There are normally two general sources of information; first, the views expressed by the people themselves and second, the observation of their behaviour. Both these sources are subject to misinterpretation. People are sometimes unable to provide a correct explanation of their activities however great their willingness to cooperate. Also, however straightforward their intentions they may, consciously or unconsciously, wish other people to have a particular view of their activities which is not in fact the correct one. Coupled with this are all the difficulties in forming an unbiased overall view from sifting reported remarks and obtaining new evidence by questioning the people concerned. Evidence from observation on the other hand has the main drawback that it is the result which is observed and not the intention. Hence the influence of other events and people must also be taken into account. This involves the specification of a model and it is this choice of specification which we are concerned with anyway.

In practice economists prefer to rely on observation rather than reported opinions largely because of the degree of subjectivity and the drawbacks experienced in previous studies, for example the Hall and Hitch (1939) investigation of pricing policies by firms. However, this does not mean that opinions of the policy-makers are without value, and in our particular instance of building society behaviour it has been possible to obtain a considerable amount of useful evidence. Since the market is dominated by the actions of a small number of large societies it is relatively easy to obtain a generally accepted assessment of building society managers' views of the aims of building societies. In addition to published statements by the Building Societies Association and individual managers it is fortunately possible to make use of the answers given by the Secretary-General of the Building Societies Association to a set of questions on the subject posed by Clayton *et al.* (1975). These two sources of information, taken together, provide the starting point for this assessment of the aims of building society behaviour. There is of course a third type of information normally available by looking at the behaviour of similar institutions. The problem is that although building societies are financial intermediaries and compete with other institutions for funds, they do not have the same sort of structure. First, as seen in Section 3.2, the composition of their lending is restricted and second, they are not ordinary commercial companies but friendly societies and hence will not necessarily operate to the same commercial criteria. In particular it is not possible to talk about profit maximization in the normal sense. There are thus substantial drawbacks to comparing building societies with other financial intermediaries and it will be more instructive to concentrate on their own behaviour in its own right in the first instance.

The societies' publicity and that of the Building Societies Association appear to concentrate on two areas: the quantity of new mortgage funds advanced and the quantity of net receipts of money invested during a given time period. These two are clear, for example, in the Building Societies Association's (1976) 'Evidence to the Housing Finance Review'. The use of gross advances is perhaps a rather misleading indicator of the societies' real concern. It is probably used largely because it is the largest numerical quantity and does not in any way imply ignorance on their part of the fact that a high turnover in housing will generate a high level of gross mortgage advances irrelevant of the change in net lending. This high level of advances will be offset by a high level of repayments of principal as house purchasers terminate the mortgage on the property they are selling before taking out a new mortgage on the property they are buying. We could, therefore, safely interpret the concern to be over the change in net lending rather than gross lending. Concern does not necessarily imply maximization, but at this stage the position can be summarized by saying that building societies appear to be concerned to have high levels of net lending in each time period as well as high levels of net receipts of savings and deposits. This is not to say that these are the only aims of building societies — there has been considerable discussion in recent years of the volume of lending to those buying a home for the first time — but that they represent the primary aims within which the other aspects of their activity can be considered. The answers obtained by Clayton *et al.* (1975) to their questions to the Secretary-General of the Building Societies Association are a little different from the foregoing conclusions largely because the 'maximization' of mortgage advances is never proffered as an objective of societies when the questions were asked. The answers given show clearly that the maximization of the rate of growth of total assets is thought to be an objective of societies, but that it must be 'qualified'. The particular qualification which is mentioned is the level of the reserve ratio with the emphasis that 'the absolute level of reserves is irrelevant; it is the ratio which is of fundamental importance'. Coupled with this is the acceptance of the objective of the maximization of the inflow of funds: 'most societies aim to maximize the inflow from investors', with the qualification, 'consistent with their ability to re-lend on mortgage and to operate with a margin to ensure that their reserves grow in line with assets'. Clearly from a practical point of view a society can have only a single objective function for its action and hence a single maximand otherwise there may very well be no course of action which is consistent with the two objectives taken separately, but the combining of the two is a simple task since lending is limited by the availability of funds and the desire for funds is limited by the ability to re-lend. As a result of the answers they obtained Clayton *et al.* draw a number of conclusions which summarize the position very clearly:

1. [Building societies] appear to be trying to maximize the rate of growth of mortgage assets subject to certain constraints;
2. the ratio of mortgages to total assets maintained by them appears to be a relatively stable value of just over 80 per cent;
3. the main source of net additions to outstanding mortgages and hence, given a more or less fixed ratio of these to total assets, of net additions to liquid assets is the net inflow of funds from the Personal Sector of the economy.

These conclusions lead them, not surprisingly, to develop a model to explain the allocation of the flow of funds into building societies.

The choice of any particular form of model is not however predetermined by the acceptance of the summary made by Clayton *et al.* The simple flow of funds model is not for example sufficiently complete for this purpose. It only explains the flow of liquid and mortgage assets given the values of the flow of shares and deposits and the interest rates of the competing assets (which of course includes the mortgage rate which is itself determined by the building societies).

Although the summary made by Clayton *et al.* seems very reasonable, the idea of building societies maximizing anything leads to consequent conclusions which are not always acceptable. The foremost problem is that building societies as friendly societies are not profit-making institutions in the normal sense of the word. They have a duty to both borrowers and investors and while the maximization of mortgage lending subject to various constraints may be in the interest of borrowers it is not necessarily in the interest of investors. Furthermore, the existence of the accounting identities will tend to have the result that maximization of the value of a major activity will involve maximization (or minimization) of other variables in the balance sheet. In particular it will tend to imply that some form of profit maximization is not far from thr truth. This difficulty is shown clearly by the work of Ghosh and Parkin (1972) who present a more complete model of building society behaviour, drawing largely on the work presented later in Ghosh (1974), which incorporates a slightly different interpretation of the aims of building societies. Their model explains not only the stock of liquid and mortgage assets but the size of shares and deposits also, estimating them all simultaneously in such a way that the overall constraint of the balance sheet (as shown in Table 3.2) is imposed. While they also suggest that building societies have 'a desire for growth subject to some acceptable security level', they assume that it is total assets rather than mortgage assets which is the maximand. This in itself might not lead us to expect any particularly different results if mortgages form a fairly stable proportion of total assets. However, Ghosh and Parkin feel that this maximization can best be expressed by assuming 'that societies aim to maximize the expected utility of reserves. The faster reserves grow, the faster can total assets grow, hence, a desire to grow implies a desire to accumulate reserves'. Subsequent writers, among them Clayton *et al.*, have not agreed with this interpretation. In particular, as already noted, they argue that the level of reserves itself is not important, it is the reserve ratio which matters. However, this criticism does not take account of the effect of the accounting identities. Using Table 3.2 the rate of growth g can be defined as

$$g = \frac{\text{ATOT}_t - \text{ATOT}_{t-1}}{\text{ATOT}_{t-1}} \tag{3}$$

where t denotes the time period. If RR_t, the reserve ratio, is to remain constant (or continue to hold minimum acceptable value) then maximizing g is achieved by maximizing

$$RD_t = \frac{R_t - R_{t-1}}{R_{t-1}} \qquad (4)$$

These additions to reserves, however, are in effect the rate of profit. The only way that reserves can be increased is through the margin between interest receipts and interest payments, where receipts take account of the yield on government securities and other assets whose value can vary. This in addition to charges is the way any other financial institution operates. The Ghosh and Parkin approach thus leads towards treating building societies, despite their friendly society status, as if they were normal commercial companies.

The major drawback to the Ghosh and Parkin approach is not, however, any connotation of profit-making but the lack of rigid relationships between mortgage and total assets on the one hand and reserve and total assets on the other.

It is clearly preferable to take the actual maximand as the objective rather than using an accounting consequence. Societies could easily increase their reserve ratios by charging differential mortgage interest rates or by appropriate timing of interest rate changes. The two-way link between the growth of assets and reserves is only maintained if societies keep a near constant or predictable rate of surplus.

The required reserve ratios diminish with the size of assets of a society. Hence during a period of expansion and concentration a fall in the aggregate reserve ratio is expected and observed. Any model involving the objective of the maximization of total reserves therefore has to be able to take account of the changing size and size distribution of societies. Not surprisingly Ghosh and Parkin do not do this.

It is also not surprising that there is no general agreement on the nature of building society behaviour in view of the lack of work on the subject. Revell (1973b) provides an excellent survey of the nature and working of the societies but does not attempt to estimate a model of their behaviour or test any hypotheses concerning them. The only substantial works in addition to the two already mentioned which are of direct relevance to the current enquiry are O'Herlihy and Spencer (1972) and Hadjimatheou (1976), although both the Treasury and London Business School models of the UK economy (HM Treasury (1977) and Renton (1975)) have useful sections on both building society behaviour and the housing market. Of these only Hadjimatheou tries to form an overall view of building societies aims, the others tend to take a rather more equation by equation approach. Hadjimatheou's suggestion is that building societies seek to maintain the demand and supply of mortgage advances in equilibrium at an acceptable liquidity ratio. Disequilibrium results in a movement of the liquidity ratio away from its desired value, rationing if demand exceeds supply, and in the longer run an adjustment through interest rates.

This approach is not inconsistent with Clayton *et al.*'s findings as it rests the main object of building society behaviour on mortgage advances. It also permits a straightforward estimation of that behaviour by developing equation (2) above to allow for fluctuations in the liquidity ratio from that desired.

Hadjimatheou's model is thus a simple and good approximation to building society behaviour, on the basis of Clayton *et al.*'s survey, if his contention is accepted that 16 per cent is the optimum level for the liquidity ratio throughout the period considered. However, a look at the path of the liquidity ratio in recent years (see Figure 3.1) together with the findings of the author's discussions with individual building society managers suggests that no such rigid optimum exists and mortgage and liquid assets both have different desired levels depending upon their rates of return. The developments which have occurred in the 1970s are analysed in detail in Chapter 4, but it is clear that a rather more detailed model of the components of the balance sheet is required than has so far been suggested as they do not all follow simple or rigid paths. The model developed here is therefore somewhat more complex, although the basic aim is maintained, namely that building societies wish to maximize mortgage advances, subject to (1) criteria of security, (2) satisfactory reserve and liquidity ratios and (3) a stable process of expansion.

3.4   Constraints on Lending

Taking the three constraints of criteria of security, satisfactory reserve and liquidity ratios and a stable process of expansion in order, first, societies do not lend to all those applicants who are prepared to accept the prevailing cost of a mortgage, however favourable are their reserves and liquidity positions. Although all loans are secured on a specific property (sometimes supplemented by a life insurance policy) building

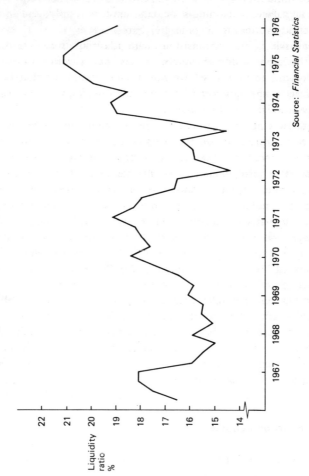

Figure 3.1 Average liquidity ratio of building societies 1967–76

Source: *Financial Statistics*

societies actually try to take all reasonable steps to avoid either any default on repayment or any depreciation of the security below the value of the debt. There are thus a set of criteria which are applied to determine the ability of the borrower to repay and the suitability of the property as security. The total sum advanced therefore is usually restricted to some multiple of between two and three times the applicant's normal salary. This entails that the applicant shall have secure prospects of a continuing income and that variable fringe payments may be excluded. This restricts the range of occupations which are considered desirable and in particular means that societies are rather unwilling to lend to unmarried women. If the application is made by a married couple, the earnings of the wife are usually given a considerably reduced weight in determining the overall sum which can be advanced. These rules are not explicit and vary between societies and over time. Not surprisingly they are used as the easiest way of imposing rationing when there is an excess demand for mortgages, although delay in the form of offering a loan to commence a month or two in the future is also widely used. In this way the society does not have to admit that it does not currently have the funds available to lend although this in itself is of course used as a reason for not providing a loan. Control of lending is also exercised by avoiding advances on the security of properties which may deteriorate. Societies prefer to lend on houses which are relatively modern and of traditional construction and they also prefer houses to flats. The older or more unsuitable the property the smaller the percentage of its value that the society is prepared to advance. This policy will affect the distribution of house prices, since the more difficult it is to raise a loan on a particular property, the lower the price, all other things being equal. Again the volume of lending can be affected by varying the percentages of the value of the property which will be advanced as a mortgage, and the value of the property is itself determined by a brief survey of the property commissioned by the society (but paid for by the applicant). All these constraints are very understandable and reflect the varying degrees of security of borrowers and their properties (or the properties they would like to purchase).

As a result of these constraints demand is in one sense always rationed so it is difficult to assess what the 'real' demand for mortgages is, even with Hadjimatheou's model. The supply constraints in the form of the reserve and liquidity ratios are rather easier to observe. The reserve ratio does not fluctuate widely in practice and as has been explained declines slowly over time with the increasing size and concentration of building societies, leaving a reasonable margin above the required minimum. The liquidity ratio on the other hand lies far above its required value, having a mean of 16.25 per cent over the period 1966—75. It also fluctuates fairly widely with a standard deviation of 1.64 per cent and a range of 13.6 to 21.1 per cent. In recent years, however, the average liquidity ratio has risen, having an average value of 17.8 per cent over the period 1970—76 (the actual time path is shown in Figure 3.1), making Hadjimatheou's assumption of a constant 16 per cent desired ratio seem rather unlikely. A clear indication can be obtained from the Clayton et al. (1975) questionnaire in which the Secretary-General of the Building Societies Association explains that: 'From a management point of view, the level of liquidity must have regard, inter alia, to forward commitments, both normal liabilities for taxation etc. and mortgages promised to would-be borrowers'. He points out that at the end of 1972 while the liquidity ratio was 16.5 per cent, if forward commitments were allowed for it was only 8.7 per cent.

If this analysis is correct, the position is now rather different, because it becomes necessary to explain not just mortgage advances but mortgage commitments as well. Far from being an unattractive prospect this puts the model on a sounder footing because the actual process of the application and agreement for a mortgage results at the time of decision in a mortgage commitment not a mortgage advance. The actual advance follows the commitment with some time lag often up to three months. Thus advances can be related to commitments by a simple distributed lag. The Secretary-General also proffers an explanation for the variation in the liquidity ratio (Clayton et al. (1975), pp. 16—17).

Broadly speaking the amount of and changes in liquidity are determined by general economic factors. In times of expected crisis, the level tends to rise in order to cope with the harder times ahead. If liquidity then runs down too much when the hard times materialize, some corrective action must be taken and the only way a society can do this is to raise its interest rates. Conversely, when societies' rates are well up to or above average, the money might flood in more quickly than it can be lent out. Lending then is stepped up; if the demand is then met (which rarely has been the case in recent times), the rates of interest would be reduced.

The existence of these general economic factors does not contradict the basic correctness of Hadjimatheou's model, for changes in the inflow of funds affected both lending and the liquidity ratio directly; however, the anticipation of difficulties by movements of the liquidity ratio in the opposite direction to the inflow of funds does require an alteration. If liquidity ratios rise if the expected inflow of funds is falling perhaps through interest rates becoming less competitive or incomes not rising so rapidly, then it is going to be very difficult to explain lending on Hadjimatheou's basis alone and a demand function for liquid assets by building societies will probably be required.

This leads directly to a further constraint of a reasonable rate of return, and I am extremely grateful to Brian Sims of the Bristol and West Building Society for the development of this point. Societies normally operate within a fairly rigid margin between interest rates offered to investors and interest rates charged to borrowers. This enables the calculation of the surplus and hence the development of reserves and the ability to increase lending to be undertaken on a fairly straightforward basis. If this margin is affected, by, say, government pressure of the mortgage rate or changed competitive behaviour on the part of the clearing banks, the whole basis of operation is altered and societies must seek a redistribution of their assets to maintain a viable pattern of mortgage lending. In particular, this led in 1973 to a move towards greater liquidity as the rate of return on liquid assets, such as local authority loans, began to exceed that on mortgages. Societies therefore chose short-run liquidity as a means of increasing long-run mortgage lending instead of having a lower rate of surplus and hence lower rate of growth given the fairly stable behaviour of the reserve ratio.

The third constraint of a stable growth path is also related to the remarks on the level of the liquidity ratio. To some extent building societies will use their liquidity to iron out fluctuations rather than responding rapidly to changes in the inflow of funds by changes in lending. This enables them either to have the time to change their interest rates or to wait until a brief fluctuation has passed. This use of the liquidity ratio to absorb short-run fluctuations reflects the unwillingness of societies to change their interest rates if it can be avoided. Most building societies adopt the rates of interest which are recommended by the Council of the Building Societies Association. The Council meets ten times a year (although it can meet on other occasions if the need arises) and recommendations for changes are made

at these meetings. The rates to savers can be changed quickly with relatively little administrative difficulty as the societies do not have to seek
the agreement of savers and usually inform them of the change at the
next convenient opportunity, for example, when the annual report is
sent out or when notification is made of the interest payable. The
mortgage rates on the other hand are more inconvenient to alter and
changes take much longer to implement. Societies normally have rules
about how much notice they must give to mortgagors of the change and
then there will be a further lag whose length will vary depending upon
the method of payment used. Direct-debiting can be altered fairly
rapidly whereas standing orders at banks have to be altered by specific
action of the borrowers themselves and it is this method of payment
which is normally used. The new rate of interest will in most cases have
immediate effect for borrowers obtaining a mortgage advance after the
change is announced, so the speed of adjustment to the new mortgage
interest rate will be greater the faster the turnover in the housing
market. The reluctance of societies to change interest rates unless
absolutely necessary is not surprising in the face of these difficulties,
not to mention the cost of sending out several million notifications.

The factors influencing the rates of interest recommended by building societies are two-fold. In the first place societies are competitors
with other financial institutions for funds and hence their inflow of
funds will be affected by movements in the rates of interest offered by
their competitors. Second societies need to have a margin between the
rates offered to savers and those charged to borrowers, so that they can
pay their expenses — wages, salaries, office expenses, etc. — and so that
they can make a surplus which can be added to reserves to allow future
expansion in mortgage lending. In practice this margin has remained
very stable, so the overall structure and movement in building society
interest rates is thus very straightforward. If the rate of interest offered
by societies to savers becomes out of line because competing interest
rates have changed, the inflow of funds will be affected. Although
changes in this inflow will initially only affect the liquidity ratios of the
societies it will eventually feed through to the level of lending. Since
societies tend to prefer a fairly stable growth of lending this will entail
a change in the savings rate to return to the equilibrium market position. The maintenance of a stable margin between the mortgage and
savings rates will then require that the mortgage rate should follow
the change in the savings rate.

The nature of the competing institutions will depend upon the
available choice of forms in which savers can hold their wealth. This

will be affected by the type of saver, whether a person, or an institution, by the size of savings which can be allocated (building societies impose a limit of £15,000 on each individual, although of course one person can hold accounts with several societies) and by the reason for saving. These reasons may vary from the desire to keep a transactions balance to a simple speculative motive. Furthermore, since interest rates are different for those who pay no tax and taxpayers in different tax brackets, it is not possible to produce a simple and generally applicable list of competitive assets. The concern over tax rates is particularly important as the building society interest rate to savers is paid net of a composite rate of tax agreed between the societies and the Inland Revenue. This tax is not reclaimable by non-taxpayers and those on rates of tax above the standard rate are liable for further taxation to bring the tax paid up to the appropriate higher rate. As a result of these difficulties we can only use general indicators of the relative level of building society interest rates to savers, by comparison with those offered on deposit accounts by commercial banks, investment accounts by the Post Office and accounts with the Trustee Savings Banks. The interest rate on less liquid assets is probably best indicated by the rate for Local Authority Loans.

The inflow of funds will vary in the main according to the behaviour of two groups. On the one hand, the large majority of accounts is held by small savers who do not change the size of their holdings substantially. They use the building societies as a means of keeping their wealth in a readily accessible liquid form. The traditional pattern is that the accounts are built up in youth to provide a deposit for house purchase where the mortgage loan is often obtained from the same society. Accounts are built up again through the rest of adult working life and used to finance special large purchases, and are then run down in retirement. The second major group, however, is the holders of large balances, who although much smaller in number are important in terms of the value of their holdings. These savers are much more sensitive to relative interest rates and it is their behaviour which affects the fluctuations in the inflow of funds more closely.

In the light of this information on the constraints on lending the aims of building societies can be summarized in a way which enables us to develop a model of their behaviour:

1. Building societies' primary aim is to advance mortgages and hence to meet demand as far as possible at the prevailing interest rates
2. The primary determinant of the level of lending is the inflow of

funds from depositors for which building societies are a competitor with other financial institutions

3. Lending is constrained by:
   a. a desire for virtually riskless lending
   b. the need to maintain reserve and liquidity ratios at levels which will enable all short-run fluctuations in the flow of funds to be absorbed without having to affect lending dramatically in order to adhere to the required levels of these ratios. (The desired liquidity will also be affected by external factors which change the relative rates of return on mortgage and liquid assets)
   c. a desire that the growth path of lending be relatively stable. (Both these last two requirements have of course been broken in practice in the 1970s)
   d. the structure of interest rates is relatively rigid and difficult to change in the short-run.

4 The Experience of the 1970s

The last two chapters have set out the structure of the housing market and the behaviour of building societies in the UK as they appear during the last twenty to twenty-five years. The suggested relations which are empirically estimated and tested in chapter 5 are derived in the main from a period of stable behaviour between 1955 and 1970. Since 1970 that stability has been substantially disrupted and the relations set out become more obscure and difficult to disentangle. As it is the purpose of this book to explain what caused this disruption and in particular what caused the rapid rise in house prices and what rôle building societies' actions played in that rise, this chapter explains what it was that happened in the 1970s.

The general pattern is fairly simple to explain — house prices began to rise more rapidly in 1971 and then rose very rapidly during 1972 and 1973 to reach a peak in 1974, since when they have risen much more slowly. During the same period building society mortgage lending also doubled, but after a peak in 1973 it fell back substantially in 1974 only to reach three times the 1971 level of new advances by 1975. However these two factors cannot be taken in isolation as the first half of the 1970s also saw unprecedented rises in incomes and in the general rate of inflation which reached a peak rather later in 1975. Thus the relative position of house prices has moved widely. Associated with the high rates of general inflation have been exceptional rates of interest which reached their maxima in 1974 and 1975 (a further peak was reached in 1976, but this lies outside our period of observation). These rates not surprisingly had substantial effects on both the demand for funds and the supply of funds for lending. While the general concern regarding the value of variables measured in money terms during this period has been with rapid rises, the concern over the volume of new housing has been very much the opposite, with it falling from a

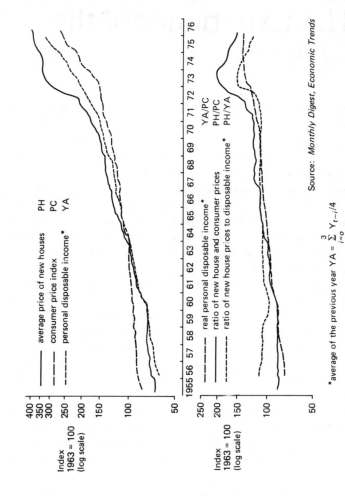

Index
1963 = 100
(log scale)

400
350
300

250

200

150

100

50

— average price of new houses   PH
— — consumer price index   PC
— - — personal disposable income*   YA

1955 56 57 58 59 60 61 62 63 64 65 66 67 68 69 70 71 72 73 74 75 76

Index
1963 = 100
(log scale)

250

200

150

100

50

— — real personal disposable income*
—— ratio of new house and consumer prices
— - — ratio of new house prices to disposable income*

YA/PC
PH/PC
PH/YA

*average of the previous year $YA = \sum_{i=0}^{3} Y_{t-i}/4$

Source: *Monthly Digest, Economic Trends*

Figure 4.1 House prices, inflation and incomes

46

small peak in 1971—72 to levels 25 per cent lower in 1974 and 1975. The timing and magnitude of these various rises and falls are crucially important for the determination of the causes of the rise in house prices and the rôle of building society lending in that rise. We shall therefore now go on to consider the whole pattern in detail so that the circumstances to be analysed are completely clear, starting with the rise in house prices.

4.1   The Rise in House Prices

During the 1960s and late 1950s the average price of new private housing increased steadily albeit slowly, with an annual average rise of 5.6 per cent fluctuating between 0.7 per cent in 1959 and 10.0 per cent in 1961. At the same time consumer prices in general increased by only 3.0 per cent per year so that over the years 1955 to 1970 the ratio of house prices to all consumer prices increased on average by 2.5 per cent per year. This rise was not uniform and the pattern can be seen in Figure 4.1. In particular the ratio remained virtually unchanged between 1955 and 1959, and only rose by 1.5 per cent a year at the end of the period between 1966 and 1970.

The movement during the 1970s is however of a very different character. Between 1971 and 1973 house prices rose dramatically by a total of 129 per cent, but this movement came to a peak in the first quarter on 1974 and prices actually fell in the second quarter of that year. The transition from the steady inflation of the 1960s to the rapid inflation of the 1970s is extremely quick, the year on year increase moving from 5.2 per cent in the last quarter of 1970 to 52.4 per cent in the first quarter of 1973.

Subsequent to 1973 house prices have again risen although at a lower rate with rises of 5.3 per cent in 1974 and 9.5 per cent in 1975, although this movement largely ceased in 1976. It is not sufficient to consider house prices in isolation from the movements in the general price level, as it would not be unreasonable to expect them to be influenced by the general trend. However, as is clear from Figure 4.1 the pattern of their development compared with the general price level (as represented by the deflator of consumers' expenditure) is very different. The increase in the general rate of inflation comes rather later, moving from 7.6 per cent in 1971 to 22.0 per cent in 1975 with rises of 6.7, 8.8 and 15.3 per cent in each of the intervening years.

Consequently the very rapid increases in house prices in 1971 to 1973 represent a very rapid relative increase, while the rises in 1974 to 1976 represent relative falls. Had house prices shown the same annual percentage change during the 1970s as they had during the 1950s and 1960s relative to the overall level of consumer prices then we would have expected to observe a value of 357.5 in the first quarter of 1976 compared with the 400.0 which was actually observed. It is thus clear that although relative house prices have moved down compared with their peak levels, they have not completed the return to the previous position. It is the primary interest of this book to explain why this divergence of the price of houses took place and whether it represents a long-run change in the determination of house prices or merely a short-run change from the previous path. Not surprisingly it is quite impossible to obtain an answer merely by inspecting the time series of price movements.

4.2   The Prices of Other Houses

It was implicitly assumed in Section 4.1 that the average price of new houses is a good indicator of house prices in general. While it suffers from some obvious drawbacks it is straightforward to show that it is a reasonable indicator. The drawbacks are mainly that not all houses are new houses and secondly that there is no such single representative dwelling which can be described as the 'average house'. In any case there is no particular price for a given dwelling as prices vary not just by regions in the country, but also by the nature of their site, even on the same estate. These last two problems are encountered with some degree of severity in the construction of almost all index numbers, the relation between the price of the new and the secondhand product is however very much specific to the housing market. As was noted in Chapter 2 the reason for concentrating on new housing is largely pragmatic, adequate figures on turnover of existing housing do not exist except for very recent years.

The familiarity of a problem does not of course mean that it is thereby unimportant. Table 4.1 shows the degree of variation between the regions in the UK. In 1972 and 1973 the average price of houses at the mortgage completion stage in the Yorkshire and Humberside region was less than half that in Greater London. Moreover, these discrepancies are not constant in relative terms through time, as can be

Table 4.1. Average regional house prices at mortgage completion

	Northern	Yorks. and Humber	East Midlands	East Anglia	Greater London	South East (excl. GLC)	South West	West Midlands	North West	Wales	Scotland	Northern Ireland
(a) Prices £												
1970	3,942	3,634	3,966	4,515	6,882	6,223	4,879	4,490	4,184	4,434	5,002	4,387
1971	4,389	4,023	4,390	4,968	7,397	7,284	5,564	4,926	4,494	4,803	5,407	4,650
1972	5,413	4,880	5,621	7,031	11,113	9,914	7,771	6,232	5,724	5,935	6,223	4,934
1973	7,414	7,059	8,191	9,849	14,447	13,164	10,868	8,775	7,836	8,382	8,595	6,181
1974	8,444	8,202	9,191	10,974	14,857	13,946	11,549	10,118	8,890	9,401	9,775	8,710
1975	9,611	9,013	9,989	11,909	14,918	14,664	11,932	10,634	9,771	10,083	11,139	10,023
(b) Prices as a % of the Greater London price												
1970	57.3	52.8	57.6	65.6	100.0	90.5	70.9	65.2	60.8	64.4	72.7	63.7
1971	59.3	54.4	59.3	67.2	100.0	98.5	75.2	66.6	60.8	64.9	73.1	62.9
1972	48.7	43.9	50.6	63.3	100.0	89.2	69.9	56.1	51.5	53.4	56.0	44.4
1973	51.3	48.9	56.7	68.2	100.0	91.1	72.2	60.7	54.2	58.0	59.5	42.8
1974	56.8	55.2	61.9	73.9	100.0	93.9	77.7	68.1	59.8	63.3	65.8	58.6
1975	64.4	60.4	67.0	79.8	100.0	98.3	80.0	71.3	65.5	67.6	74.7	67.2
(c) Rate of change of prices %												
1970	6.1	5.8	4.6	5.0	11.1	7.4	8.5	3.3	6.7	6.4	8.5	11.3
1971	11.3	10.7	10.7	10.0	7.5	17.0	14.0	9.7	7.4	8.3	8.1	6.0
1972	23.3	21.3	28.0	41.5	50.2	36.1	39.7	26.5	27.4	23.6	15.3	6.1
1973	37.0	44.7	45.7	40.0	30.0	32.8	39.9	40.8	36.9	41.2	37.9	25.3
1974	13.9	16.2	12.2	11.4	2.8	5.9	6.3	15.3	13.5	12.2	13.7	40.9
1975	13.8	9.9	8.7	8.5	0.4	5.1	3.3	5.1	9.9	7.3	14.0	15.1

Source: Building Societies Association, *Facts and Figures*

seen from Table 4.1 (b). The rate of change of house prices varies between the different parts of the country. The pattern shown in Table 4.1 (c) suggests that the inflation in prices started in London earlier than it did elsewhere, and levelled off earlier as well. Table 4.1 (b) shows that although the differences between prices increased in 1972, by 1975 the general dispersion of prices had been considerably reduced with East Anglia, the East Midlands and the South West experiencing the highest relative rises in price and the distinction between prices in Greater London and the South East being virtually eliminated. The weighting problem arising from this is simply the choice of quantity weights to be applied to each region in the calculation of the average price for the country as a whole.

The variability in the composition of the housing constructed in each time period presents a rather more difficult problem. Not only are there variations between the quantities of different sorts of dwellings, flats, maisonettes, two-bedroomed houses, detached houses, etc. which will affect the average price but the quality of these dwellings is not constant either. Changes in size of rooms, nature of construction materials and types of facilities — baths, central heating, cupboards etc. — for example can have an important impact on the price of what is ostensibly the same type of dwelling. The quality of housing has risen steadily over time and Needleman's (1965) estimates suggest that this represents an annual rate of change in value of approximately 4 per cent which, on the basis of the previous section, would suggest that during the 1950s and 1960s the large majority of the rise in house prices was due to increases in quality. The price index used in Figure 4.1 takes no account of this, and therefore in so far as the consumer price index represents a constant quality index, the relative movement in house prices is overstated. It also entails that any counting of the number of houses as a means of estimating the quantity of output of housing will tend to be an understatement as the quality per unit rises. Putting it another way, the value of constant price 'housing services' which are consumed rises.

There is a further underlying aspect to the problem in that the information obtained on house prices is only a sample drawn from houses mortgaged with building societies. In using it, it must be assumed that the properties mortgaged with the societies are a reasonable cross-section of new properties constructed. Given the size of the sample and the fact that this concerns new houses alone, this is not an unreasonable assumption, although the distribution of house type and geographical location will vary from quarter to quarter.

The use of new house prices, with the qualifications that have just been made, as a satisfactory indicator of all house prices rests on the fact that movements in new and other house prices follow the same course. Since an index is being used, the absolute level is not important. This relation is the more likely because it is the market for existing housing which is the most important. If the price of new houses moves out of line with that of existing houses there is a very large number of close substitutes among existing houses, hence deviations in relative terms will tend to be small except under conditions of changing tastes or perhaps excess supply when builders prefer to hold out at a higher price in the hope of a future rise.

4.3   Prices Relative to Incomes

Since the price index of new houses is not of constant quality some of the rise in price may merely reflect rising real incomes and hence the ability to buy higher quality housing without any reduction in the consumption of other products. Boléat (1976) stresses this view when trying to point to the long-run behaviour of house prices. He considers

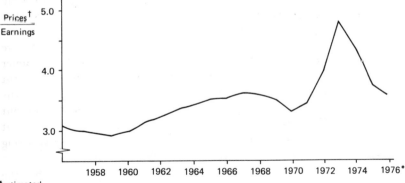

*estimated
†new house prices at approval stage
average earnings of fully employed men
aged 21 and over drawn from *New Earnings Survey* (basic weekly wage rate
of manual workers, *Economic Trends*, prior to 1963)
Source: Building Societies Association, *Facts and Figures*, no. 7.

Figure 4.2   The ratio of new house prices to average earnings

the ratio of house prices to earnings showing that by 1975 the ratio was returning to the level it held during the 1960s. Moreover he also points out (Figure 4.2) that house prices were relatively low compared with earnings in the years immediately prior to 1971 and hence that some of the impetus for the rapid rise in prices can be attributed to this. In effect he argues that the previous years represent a disequilibrium so that when a movement to return towards equilibrium began there was an incentive for it to continue and even to accelerate. Clearly in assessing this view other factors must be taken into account since it is by no means clear that earnings rather than personal disposable income is the determining factor, and no account is taken of movements in interest rates or supply factors which have some rôle to play. It is however useful in drawing attention to the contribution of income and the existence of historically low prices in the period immediately preceding the rapid inflation. The general picture is set out in the lower graph of Figure 4.1, where although the ratio of new house prices to consumer prices has risen consistently up to 1974, the ratio of new house prices to disposable incomes remained fairly constant before the 1970s.

4.4   House Prices and the Building Cycle

Moving to another aspect of the housing market, while price has been varying the quantity of new construction had not remained stable either. In this case, however, as noted in Chapter 2 (see Figure 2.1), there is no historical stability to this variable. Although the maximum number of new private houses completed occurred in 1968 the expansion of housebuilding had really ended in 1964 and the position has been one of decline since 1968 with a small recovery in 1971–73. This therefore presents a further problem in analysis, as although there was considerable demand pressure for housing in the early 1970s the response of supply was fairly limited. Under normal circumstances it would be expected that a rapid rise in price for a product would encourage a substantial increase in its supply.

A very clear exposition of the behaviour up to 1973 can be found in the report by Neuberger and Nichol (1976) published by the Department of the Environment on land and property prices. This report has a wider coverage than our current concerns but it provides some useful information which is not otherwise available, in particular concerning planning applications and figures for turnover from estate agents' returns. A clear picture can therefore be built up of the response of supply to the increase in house prices.

In order to meet an increase in demand housebuilders can take a number of steps. First, they can speed up the process of construction and hence increase the number of completions in the short-run. Second, they can actually build more houses in the sense that the number of starts is increased, but this will only feed through to com-

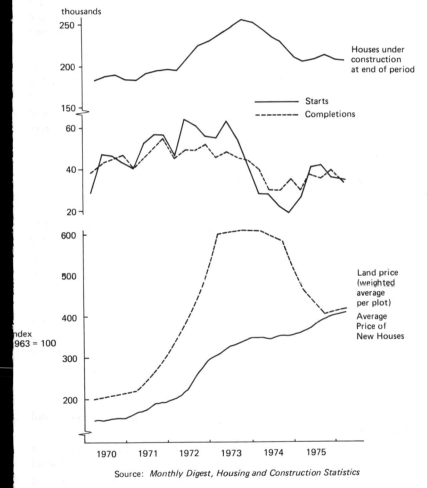

Source: *Monthly Digest, Housing and Construction Statistics*

Figure 4.3   Private housebuilding in the 1970s

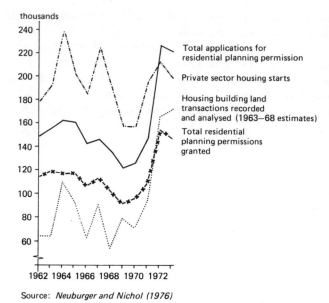

Source: *Neuburger and Nichol (1976)*

Figure 4.4   Housing starts, land transactions and planning permissions
for England and Wales

pletions with a lag. Third, it is not possible to start building without
first purchasing the land and obtaining planning permission for it.
Figures 4.3 and 4.4 show that all these responses actually occurred
during the early 1970s, but that the lags in the system meant that the
boom was largely over before an adequate supply response could occur.
Housing starts respond far more strongly to the cyclical pattern in
demand, remaining above completions from early 1971 until the end of
1973 and falling below completions during 1974 and the early part of
1975. This shows that starts follow the price pattern very closely, but
completions on the other hand are rather sluggish which results in a
substantial increase in the number of houses under construction in
1972 and 1973. Thus builders' initial intentions follow what one would
expect from prices, but this is not fully carried through to sales on the
market. Planning applications react even more strongly than housing
starts but this is to be expected since the investment involved is not
necessarily so substantial. The reason for the sluggish response of
completions is not clear for although costs rose rapidly during the same
period, profitability also increased. Land prices formed a major compo-

nent of the rise in costs and according to Neuberger and Nichol a third of this rise was attributable to the inability of planning authorities to expand the granting of permission sufficiently fast. It is clear from Figure 4.4 that the ratio of planning permission granted to applications falls during 1972 and 1973. However, this is only to be expected under conditions of expansion as applicants will tend to put forward less viable schemes under pressure. The landprice series shown in Figure 4.3 has the characteristics normally associated with a speculative boom; it starts rising earlier in 1971 and then rises much faster during 1972 and 1973, but rises further than can be sustained and prices then drop until the end of 1975. By the end of the period the land cost component has actually fallen compared with overall house prices, reflecting the general increase in all other costs, most especially labour.

New construction only forms a part of the total housing stock, but Figure 4.5 shows that the demand pressure on new housing existed for all housing between late 1970 and early 1973. Although the number of sales does not vary substantially the ease of sale increases rapidly up to May 1972, as is indicated by both the average number of houses on sale and the average number on sale for more than three months. Not surprisingly this sequence follows the pattern of house prices very closely.

The general picture of the housing market is thus that while there is some matching rise in the number of houses on which construction is begun when prices rose this rise does not pass through to completions and hence the rise in supply is much weaker than the rise in demand. This in itself can be expected to be a contributory factor to the rise in house prices. We cannot suggest what we would have expected to happen in response to a rise in prices until we can estimate supply functions for private housing as suggested in Chapter 2. The general form of those relations was that completions were largely dependent upon previous starts with only a relatively small effect by other factors, such as a price, on the speed of construction. Starts on the other hand are affected by price and the more usual parameters of an economic supply function (see pp. 24—5).

Thus far therefore it appears that the early 1970s showed that at the outset house prices were if anything rather below the level which would have been expected on the basis of historical trends with respect to disposable income and the general price level. However during 1972 and 1973 prices rose rapidly to levels which were much higher than is consistent with previous trends in either of these variables, although by

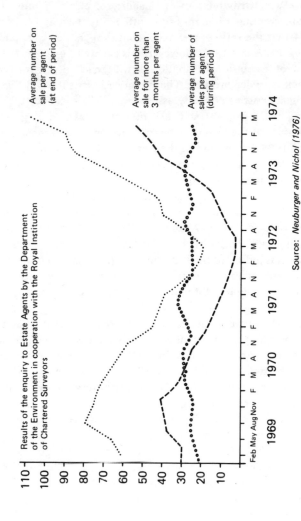

Figure 4.5 The market for existing houses: estate agent's returns

Source: *Neuburger and Nichol (1976)*

1976—77 the rapid general price inflation had largely restored the pattern. The quantity of housebuilding on the other hand did not respond strongly to a rise in price, and to some extent the decline in housebuilding since 1968 may have contributed to a relative shortage of housing.

The major causes of the rise in house prices therefore appear to lie elsewhere. In particular it is necessary to consider the behaviour of the rest of the housing market by looking at the public sector and at the effects of government policy in general and examining the development of building society behaviour, as that is the major motivation of this study. However, government behaviour will be taken first.

4.5   The Rôle of Government Policy

Governments have affected the housing market in several different ways as discussed in Chapter 1. Three types of policy can be distinguished: first, policy affecting the public sector of the housing market directly either by changing the quantity of the stock or the price (rent) of housing; second, policy affecting the private sector of the housing market as a primary aim, legislative changes in security of tenure, low-interest rate loans to building societies for example; third, general changes in public policy such as budgetary changes, affecting, say, income tax rates or the demand for the output of the non-housing part of the construction industry, which will have an indirect effect on the housing market. The 1970s witnessed changes in all these areas, and all these must be taken into account in forming the final assessment of the determinants of the rise in house prices.

Considering the public sector of the housing market first, it was noted in Chapter 2 that housebuilding in the public sector tended to follow the same general pattern as housebuilding in the private sector (see Figure 2.1, for example). The same is not true of the 1970s. Public sector housebuilding fell from 1970 to 1972 and then rose as a deliberate attempt to counteract the downturn of supply in 1974. This is shown in Figure 4.6 where the private and public sectors are contrasted. At the end of the period in 1976 the pattern is beginning to move the other way with limits on local authority expenditure beginning to affect the number of new houses started as inflation in prices continues.

The supply of local authority houses is also affected by the number of sales of their dwellings, usually to sitting tenants. During the 1960s

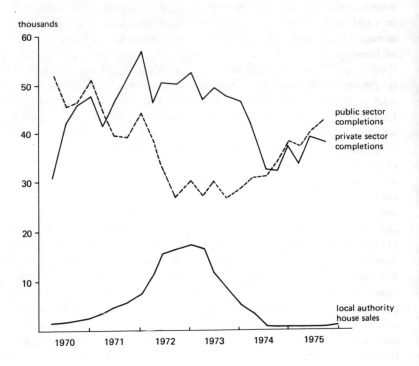

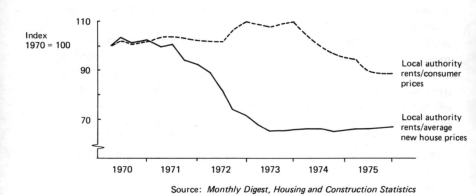

Source: *Monthly Digest, Housing and Construction Statistics*

Figure 4.6   The public sector of the housing market
in the 1970s (quarterly)

sales were always fairly small and trivial in comparison with new construction, but with the advent of the Conservative administration in 1970 sales were encouraged and the sales for 1972 alone exceeded those sold between 1963 and 1969. These sales ended with the defeat of the government in the first election of 1974 and sales in 1975 were lower than in any of the previous twelve years. These sales are shown in Figure 4.6 on the same scale as new construction so that their relative importance is clear. As is shown in the empirical analysis of Chapter 5 these sales have only a limited effect on the market as a whole.

Local authorities and the government not only control the quantity of public sector housing, but also its price. While it is the local authority which actually determines the rent there are government controls on the maximum size of increases which may be implemented and directives on the degree of subsidy which may be given. The nature and impact of these measures is discussed in Mayes and Stafford (1977). Rents have been subsidized throughout the period, but as shown in Figure 4.6 they have not followed the pattern of house prices, but rather more the general level of inflation until the period of really rapid inflation after 1974 when their relative position improved. This is perhaps surprising because to a large extent local authority housing costs have followed private sector prices. However, this issue was outside our current concerns. What is important is that the cost of renting from the public sector has not acted as an incentive to move into the private sector rather the opposite, a relative price advantage has built up in favour of local authority tenants.

Public policy affecting other parts of the housing sector is much more difficult to assess. There are particular elements of legislation, such as the Housing Finance Act, 1972 and the Rent Act, 1974. The 1972 Act attempted to alter the basis of subsidization of local authority housing and had some upward effect on rents and downward effect on the number of local authority dwellings. It also increased the scope of the 'fair rent' scheme and expanded the granting of rent allowances in the private sector, thus giving a greater weight to the support of low income families in the private sector. The general effect of this and the 1974 Act which extended controls further in the private sector has been to reduce the amount of rented accommodation available at the lower end of the market. In 1972 there was an increased move by tenants to leave the local authority sector because of fears about the size of rises in rents (see Building Societies Association, 1976); fears which were later shown to be exaggerated. The general effect of the 1974 Act which extended controls further in the private sector was to reduce the amount of rented accommodation available at the lower end of the market. The overall implications for the owner-occupied sector are relatively small as both supply and demand will be increased as both landlords and tenants shift their form of tenure.

The other policy is more direct. The £500 million loan made available to building societies at a favourable rate of interest in April 1974 for a year was of far more direct impact, and as we shall see in Section 4.6, provided liquidity for societies at a time when the inflow of funds was at a very low level. This enabled societies to hold the mortgage rate at the then exceptionally high level of 11 per cent. Since this loan is quantified it is possible to take it into account explicitly in the analysis in Chapter 5, but the effects of government pressure on interest rates are much more difficult to deal with as they have no quantifiable value. On the whole they must reluctantly be consigned to the unknown residual in this explanation and the success of the analysis can be judged from the size of this residual.

The third category of overall government policy is also difficult to incorporate. Income taxation is included through its effect on personal disposable incomes. There the major effects are through the change in the system of allowances in 1974 and the increases in rates in 1975 and 1976. The general economic picture as shown by gross domestic product at constant factor cost is modest expansion by 1.6 per cent in 1971 and 2.9 per cent in 1972, rapid expansion in 1973 by 5.7 per cent and thereafter contraction, by 0.8 per cent in 1974 and 1.6 per cent in 1975. This again can be incorporated directly into any estimation as can the effects of the Conservative three-stage prices and incomes policy of 1972 to 1974 and the Social Contract of 1975 to 1977. It is the degree of which the parameters of economic behaviour change rather than the variables on which it is based which is so difficult to incorporate. The main point to note concerning the economic cycle in the economy as a whole is that it follows the cycle in the housing market rather than precedes it. The three-stage prices and incomes policy was designed to prevent inflation getting out of hand at a time of expansion and in the first two phases involved the control of many prices including rents. The 1975 to 1977 policy on the other hand was designed with the twin aims of holding down inflation and maintaining employment at a time of contraction, so their effects cannot be expected to be similar.

Before leaving the subject of government policy its effects on the money markets as well as on real development should be considered, since the flow of funds is crucial to the explanation of building society lending. In so far as policy affects interest rates this will feed through the money market eventually to building society interest rates, and this will occur whether the government tried to influence the rate of interest or the size of the money supply. As is noted in Section 4.6 the major feature of interest rate behaviour in the 1970s is the surge in interest rates in 1973 to 1974. The concern at this point, however, is over the indirect effects of policy on behaviour, the most important of which is the introduction of the code of Competition and Credit Control in late 1971. These measures were not aimed at building societies at all but were designed by the Bank of England to facilitate two aims: first, an increase in the level of competition between banks both as borrowers and lenders; and second the control by the Bank over the movements in UK financial markets. In the first case clearing banks tended to operate as a cartel, offering the same rates of interest and similar patterns of lending, the idea was to break this down and offer a better service to lenders and borrowers by permitting freer competition. In so far as banks were successful in increasing competition building societies would also be affected where they were competing for the same funds. It is difficult to say what the actual effects have been, but it is made clear in the next section that the pattern of interest rates has been much more variable since 1971 than it was before. The problem, of course, is to distinguish between the effects of high interest rates, which are themselves relatively unpredictable because of their novelty and the effect of the change in competitive conditions. Let us proceed therefore at this stage to consider building societies and their reactions to interest rate changes in the 1970s.

4.6   Building Society Lending in the 1970s

The flow of funds into and out of building societies experienced fluctuations which were on the same sort of scale experienced by house prices. Table 4.2 shows that the inflow of funds into building societies doubled between the first quarter of 1971 and the second quarter of 1973. Receipts then fell back again in the latter part of the year and in early 1974 but by the second quarter of 1975 they were three times their 1971 level. Receipts do not reflect the funds available to building

Table 4.2. Building society shares and deposits in the 1970s (in £ million)

	Receipts	With-drawals	Net increase in shares and deposits	Total value of shares and deposits held	Total value in constant prices*
1970 Q1	675	447	280	8,914	6,899
Q2	737	468	336	9,250	7,018
Q3	815	475	395	9,645	7,139
Q4	853	477	479	10,124	7,411
1971 Q1	818	488	394	10,518	7,572
Q2	963	596	453	10,971	7,672
Q3	1,094	640	523	11,494	7,932
Q4	1,216	667	664	12,158	8,299
1972 Q1	1,310	807	579	12,737	8,543
Q2	1,334	859	574	13,311	8,798
Q3	1,289	930	439	13,750	8,952
Q4	1,363	899	601	14,351	9,094
1973 Q1	1,460	1,133	422	14,773	9,159
Q2	1,602	996	752	15,525	9,426
Q3	1,558	1,231	444	15,969	9,505
Q4	1,433	1,181	484	16,453	9,571
1974 Q1	1,434	1,455	135	16,588	9,175
Q2	1,497	1,240	474	17,062	8,999
Q3	1,680	1,292	547	17,609	8,980
Q4	1,759	1,218	837	18,446	9,150
1975 Q1	2,009	1,264	909	19,355	9,052
Q2	2,416	1,485	1,179	20,534	8,832
Q3	2,340	1,541	988	21,522	8,860
Q4	2,315	1,532	1,096	22,618	9,105
1976 Q1	2,723	1,680	1,258	23,876	9,190

*Using the consumers' expenditure deflator, PC (1963 = 100)

societies for lending as withdrawals also have to be taken into account and they do not follow the same time path as receipts. Table 4.2, therefore, shows not only receipts and withdrawals but the net change in the shares and deposits outstanding, which, as was noted in Section 3.4 is also affected by the interest credited to customers' accounts.

Naturally we would expect these series to increase with inflation irrelevant of all other considerations, but Table 4.2 also shows that in real terms the value of shares and deposits increased rapidly during the period 1970—73, although while the value in current prices continues to rise during 1974 and 1975 this is not true in real terms. The first quarter of 1974 is in a sense extraordinary as a result of the miners strike and the ensuing three-day week, so it is not surprising if the value of real shares and deposits fell during that period. It is noticeable that receipts are relatively low in both the first and second quarters of 1974 and that withdrawals are unusually high in the first quarter. In fact the first quarter is the only occasion that withdrawals actually exceed receipts. Although, in current values, the net increase in shares and deposits reaches an historic maximum again in the fourth quarter of 1974, the effects of general inflation are seen very clearly in the value of total shares and deposits in constant prices. In mid-1975 the real values are down to levels experienced in mid-1972, and despite record inflows of funds at double the 1972 levels the recovery by 1976 is still very limited. If we consider these shares and deposits in terms of funds for house purchase the pattern would be rather different as the main rise in prices occurs earlier in 1971—73. However, since the inflation in house prices was even larger than general inflation the inference is even stronger that the real lending ability of building societies fell during this period. This is reflected in the actual lending shown in Table 4.3. Overall, however, as was shown in Chapter 3, the building societies have been taking an increasing share of private savings.

Following the rises and falls in the flow of funds into building societies mortgage commitments and hence advances have shown similar fluctuations. Cross advances reflect both the net increase in advances and the turnover of houses among existing mortgagors, hence the net figures shown in Table 4.3 more accurately reflect the response of building societies to the increase in the supply of funds. At the same time the prices of houses were rising so current price values of the new advances will over-estimate their impact in the sense of number and type of mortgaged dwellings. Table 4.3 therefore also presents the number of new commitments and the value of net new advances deflated by the price of housing and by the consumers' expenditure deflator. These show very different features from the raw data. In particular they show that while in both current values and constant consumer prices the peak period of lending appears to be between the second quarter of 1972 and the first quarter of 1973, in constant house prices it lies earlier between the third quarter of 1971 and the third quarter of 1972. This is clear from both the last column of Table 4.3 and from numbers of mortgage commitments with, as was explained in Chapter 3, a lead of around three months. Thus while lending in constant and current prices in 1973 was, respectively, 48 per

Table 4.3. Building society lending in the 1970s (in £ million)

	Mortgage advances	Increase in mortgages outstanding	Ratio of net to gross mortgage advances	Mortgage commitments*	Value of increase in mortgages outstanding at constant prices†	Value of increase in mortgages outstanding in constant house prices‡
1970 Q1	384	201	0.52	457 (130)	156	129
2	497	269	0.54	561 (153)	204	170
3	568	310	0.55	586 (156)	229	191
4	572	308	0.54	584 (156)	225	189
1971 Q1	509	289	0.57	626 (157)	208	167
2	677	393	0.58	777 (190)	275	221
3	786	468	0.60	819 (191)	323	245
4	786	450	0.57	791 (179)	307	230
1972 Q1	769	465	0.60	937 (196)	312	226
2	925	571	0.62	1,079 (210)	377	250
3	1,020	632	0.62	933 (170)	411	234
4	935	547	0.59	853 (152)	347	187
1973 Q1	993	644	0.65	968 (156)	399	205
2	878	500	0.57	797 (127)	304	152
3	915	503	0.55	843 (130)	299	148
4	754	352	0.47	646 (99)	205	101
1974 Q1	624	318	0.51	519 (81)	176	92
2	553	242	0.44	631 (102)	128	70
3	803	415	0.52	952 (147)	212	117
4	970	515	0.53	975 (141)	255	145
1975 Q1	965	534	0.55	1,095 (153)	250	146
2	1,208	653	0.54	1,357 (183)	281	170
3	1,374	768	0.56	1,383 (178)	316	196
4	1,417	812	0.57	1,394 (177)	327	206
1976 Q1	1,322	808	0.61	1,516 (180)	311	202

*figures in brackets are the number of mortgage commitments in thousands
†using the consumer's expenditure deflator, PC (1963 = 100)

cent and 84 per cent greater than the lending in 1970, in terms of the number of houses which could be purchased it was lower by 14 per cent or 11 per cent depending whether we look at commitments or the value of net advances deflated by house prices. It is, however, clear from all four measures that the low level of lending in late 1973 and early 1974 was short lived and in 1975 lending was at higher levels than ever before.

Since the main point of the current analysis is to explain the rapid rise in house prices, Tables 4.1, 4.2 and 4.3 should be considered together. For ease of comparison the major series from these three tables are graphed in Figure 4.7. Lending both in terms of values and the number of advances was increasing more rapidly from 1970 to mid-1972, than during the main period of the rise in prices, mid-1972 to 1973. Although new mortgage lending increased much more rapidly than new house prices during the 1950s and 1960s, 8.5 compared to 5.6 per cent, this cannot account for a virtual doubling of the rate of new lending in constant house or consumer prices between the first quarter of 1970 and the third quarter of 1971. There is thus *prima facie* evidence for causation in that the rise in mortgage lending precedes the rise in house prices. Although this is a sufficient condition it remains for the multivariate analysis of Chapter 5 to take into account the simultaneous movement of all the variables in the model and hence show the contribution of mortgage lending to the rise in house prices in practice. The general pattern of the two series is, however, relatively similar if the amplitude of the changes is ignored; the sharp drop in lending in 1974 corresponds with the pause in the rise in house prices. The even greater rise in lending in 1975 is not however matched by a rise in house prices of anything like the same extent. Any explanation of the rise in house prices cannot therefore rest on building society lending alone. In the period 1971–73 it seems likely that other factors have contributed to the rise in house prices as well as any contribution that many have been made by increased building society lending; whereas in 1975 house prices did not rise in line with mortgage lending and hence the presumption is that other factors contributed to ensuring this lower rate of increase.

The comparison of the paths of the inflow of funds and mortgage lending in Figure 4.7 shows that building societies were following approximately the pattern of behaviour expected in that in general lending follows the path of the inflow of funds with a lag and with less fluctuation. The most striking deviation is during the period 1972–

66

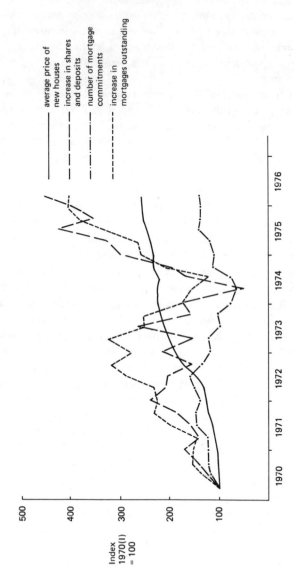

Figure 4.7 The pattern of the 1970s

average price of
new houses

increase in shares
and deposits

number of mortgage
commitments

increase in
mortgages outstanding

Index
1970(I)
= 100

500 400 300 200 100

1970 1971 1972 1973 1974 1975 1976

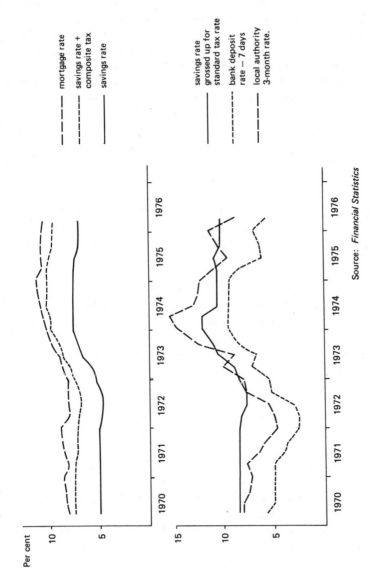

Figure 4.8 The pattern of interest rates in the 1970s

Source: *Financial Statistics*

73 when the level of new lending continued to increase although the increase in the inflow of funds had begun to fall back. The fluctuations in lending are substantial and an observable impact on the housing market can be expected. If lending does not follow the inflow of funds most of the difference will be reflected in the liquidity of societies, which also fluctuated over the period, though in a much more mild fashion. Compared with previous behaviour these fluctuations are round a rising trend, reflecting as was suggested in Chapter 3 that as a result of the interest structure prevailing in 1975 societies actually preferred to hold liquid assets to holding mortgages.

This interest rate pattern is shown in Figure 4.8. While the mortgage rate has followed the savings rate closely during the period quite wide fluctuations can be observed between the savings rate and competing rates offered by other institutions to investors. Concomitant with this is much of the fluctuation in the inflow of funds into societies, if the temporary fluctuation associated with the three-day week in the first quarter of 1974 is neglected. These fluctuations in the interest rate differential are not present in the 1950s and 1960s, although of course neither were such high interest rates either. During 1971 and the early part of 1972 interest rates moved in favour of building societies with a consequent inflow of funds. At the same time the margin between the mortgage and savings rates remained relatively high. In 1973 to 1975 however, the position was reversed with the rate for lending to local authorities at three months actually rising above the grossed up building society savings rate. In fact had not the clearing banks been compelled to keep their rates to small savers down to 9.5 per cent it is likely that their rates offered on deposit accounts at seven days would also have risen above building society rates compared with their more normal substantial adverse differential. Pressure against very high mortgage rates also contributed to a narrowing of the differential between the mortgage and savings rate for building societies. Some persistence of this unusual behaviour can be explained by the government loan of 1974 to 1975 which enabled societies to pursue an interest rate policy which would otherwise have threatened their liquidity and new lending.

To the extent that relative rather than absolute interest rate differentials should be considered Figure 4.4 exaggerates the fluctuations of the 1970s and the extent of their deviation from previous behaviour. One possible determining factor of this new behaviour in the 1970s is the introduction by the Bank of England of the new set of guidelines for behaviour in the financial sector called Competition and Credit Control in 1971. In so far as the banking system responded to these guidelines clearly the building societies would have to respond also in order to maintain their previous pattern of lending, irrelevant of any plans for increased expansion or other such changes in behaviour. In the face of such a possible structural change it would be difficult for the societies to predict what the effects of changes in the interest differential would be on the flow of funds as previous experience might no longer be a good guide. Thus wider differentials could be experienced partly as a result of the process of adaptation to the new competitive conditions and to that extent could be expected to disappear as the market becomes accustomed to the new guidelines. Additionally, since building societies cannot adjust their interest rates as rapidly to changing market conditions as can the commercial banks, there are bound to be fluctuations in differentials purely from lagged adjustment, and these differentials will be wider with more rapid changes in interest rates.

4.7   The Problem of the 1970s

The striking feature of the 1970s which has been exposed in this chapter is the very great variability of almost every aspect of the housing and building society sectors compared with the previous fifteen years. It is not merely that the price of new private housing has increased by 250 per cent in only six years, but that building society lending has doubled, halved and then tripled, interest rates have doubled, completions of private houses have fallen to levels not experienced since 1957, etc. Similar sorts of experience are observed for most of the variables considered. The problem is to identify the causes of these fluctuations and to determine how much of the explanation rests on actions within the housing and building society sector and how much stems from outside it.

The disentangling of the complex relations between the variables is not aided by the existence of circumstances in the 1970s which had not occurred during the recent past. It is thus difficult to look to past behaviour to decide upon the reactions of the market to changes in the determining variables. In particular it is difficult to estimate people's reactions to very rapid inflation as it is likely that they react rather differently to a situation which is obviously dynamic than to previous experience which is relatively static. Secondly the introduction of

Competition and Credit Control may have resulted in fundamental changes in the behaviour of the financial market at just the time that the rapid rise in house prices began. This helps to complicate the issue of the simultaneous determination of events. The exact nature of behaviour is also obscured by the existence of government intervention in the market, both in the form of legislation (for example, the Housing Finance and Rent Acts which affect the supply of housing) and by informal influence in trying to persuade building societies to hold down mortgage rates under the veiled threat of unwelcome intervention should the persuasion be ignored. These factors are very difficult to quantify and yet may be of substantial importance in the determination of some of the results.

Lastly, in analysing the 1970s it must be borne in mind that behaviour over the immediately preceding periods may be of considerable importance in the explanation of events. It cannot be assumed that the beginning of the period represents an equilibrium position, purely because there have been no violent changes. It is important to be able to consider the hypothesis that at least initially the behaviour of the 1970s was a reaction to disequilibrium which had built up during the late 1960s.

5 The Specification and Estimation of Behaviour

5.1 A Model of Building Society Behaviour and its Effects on House Prices

The previous three chapters have successively examined the structure of the housing market, the aims and nature of building society behaviour and the developments in these two sectors during the early 1970s. It is now time to present, estimate and use a model which can explain the effects of building society behaviour on house prices during the 1970s. As with all models of a fair size it is difficult to grasp the full implications of their structure at a single glance so two flowcharts, Figures 5.1 and 5.2, showing the interrelation of the housing and building society sectors and the structure of building society activity, are included to clarify the general framework.

In the centre of Figure 5.1 is the variable on which our interest revolves: the price of new houses. This price is determined by the demand and supply of new housing and hence, as in any simple market model of this form, quantity, the number of houses completed, is jointly determined with price. Commencing at the lefthand side of the figure, the number of new houses started is determined as a supply equation by the cost of construction compared with the eventual return in the form of the price of new houses, the amount of finance available for housing purchase both from building societies and other sources and the cost of finance as measured by the rate of interest charged. The variables are expressed in real terms by considering them relative to the level of consumer prices. Finally there is a simple physical constraint on housebuilding which also applies to completions as well as starts in the form of weather conditions.

Moving to the right completions are largely determined by previous starts although changes in interest rates, house prices and the weather

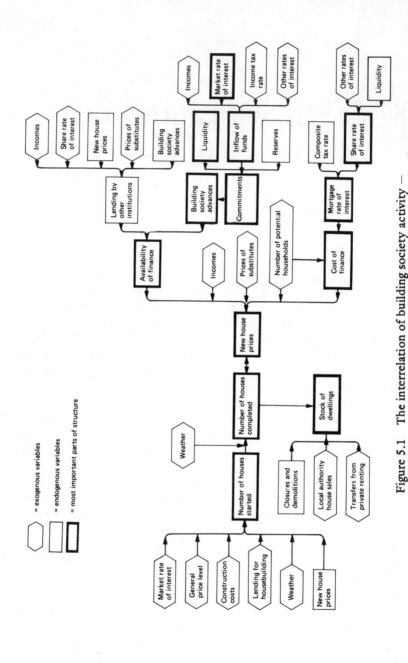

Figure 5.1 The interrelation of building society activity — the market for new houses

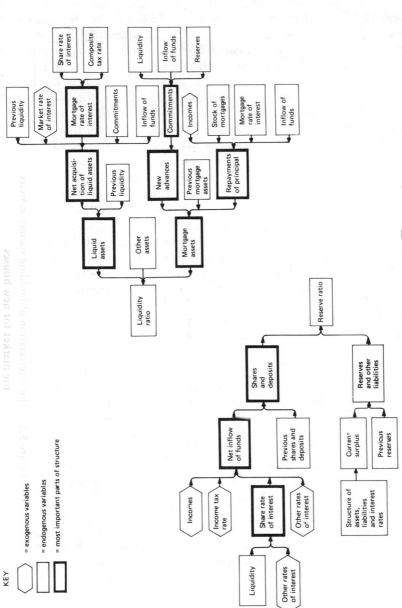

KEY

◇ = exogenous variables

▭ = endogenous variables

▮ = most important parts of structure

Figure 5.2   The structure of building society activity

affect the rate of completion. These completions add to the stock of housing, which, as is shown to its left, is also affected by closures of dwellings and transfers of dwellings from other sectors into the owner-occupied sector either by local authority sales or from the privately rented sector.

We can now move across to consider the determinants of new house prices. The demand for housing is a function of the number of potential purchasers, shown as the number of potential households. The ability of these households to purchase is affected by their incomes, the level of building society advances and the cost of borrowing. Demand is also affected by the relative price of housing both in terms of the rents charged on alternative accommodation, the expectation of future house prices and the level of consumer prices in general, referred to as prices of substitutes in Figure 5.1. Supply and demand are equated with the number of current completions and the existing stock, with due allowance for the availability of other new housing in the public sector. This completes the housing side of the model and we can now move across to consider the building society part shown on the righthand side of the figure.

The links which we have shown between the building societies and the housing market come from the level of mortgage advances via the availability of finance and the cost of finance in the form of the mortgage rate of interest. The actual level of advances on mortgage depends upon the take-up of offers of mortgage loans made by building societies, which are shown as mortgage commitments (immediately below it in the figure). It is commitments which represent the decision for the societies rather than the resulting advances and this decision is made on the basis of the funds available both from existing liquidity and from the inflow of new funds. The volume of lending which societies can undertake is also constrained by the need to have an adequate reserve ratio. The demand for borrowing on mortgage is shown simply as a function of borrowers income and the cost of borrowing.

Building societies are not the only source of finance for house purchase (although they are by far the most important for most borrowers) and a second branch of lending, shown in the top right corner of the figure is determined not only by incomes, relative prices and incomes, but by building society lending as well, because the two sources of funds tend to compensate each other.

As the interrelations in the structure of the building society sector are rather more complex they have been developed in more detail in

Figure 5.2. Figure 5.1 shows the two main linkages between the building societies and other parts of the economy.

The inflow of funds (shown on the righthand side of Figure 5.1 on the main completions, prices, commitment axis) is clearly the most important item in determining lending by societies. It is primarily composed of receipts of new shares and deposits less withdrawals of existing shares and deposits, but it is also increased by the interest on existing shares and deposits which is credited to the depositors' accounts. This last is a simple function of the stock of shares and deposits and the rate of interest payable on that stock. Moving on to consider new deposits and withdrawals, both are largely determined by the deposit rate of interest, the competing market rate of interest, tax rates and the income of those involved. The specifications of the two equations are not, however, identical.

The remaining relation shown in Figure 5.1 (bottom righthand corner) relates to building society interest rates. Since building societies are competing for funds the rate of interest offered to investors (the share rate) is primarily determined by competing market rates of interest, with the liquidity position of the societies affecting the need to change the rate, low (high) liquidity indicating the need for a rise (fall) in the share rate. The mortgage rate is adjusted to the share rate after allowance for the composite rate of tax which societies pay, thus allowing societies to make a small surplus on their operations.

This simple flowchart does not bring out clearly the ways in which the building societies themselves influence their asset and liability structure. This is shown in Figure 5.2 with the liability side of the balance sheet running from left to right and the asset side from right to left.

Taking the asset side first, the liquidity ratio is determined by the choice made by the societies between liquid assets, mortgage assets and other assets largely in the form of branches and other premises. These other assets are determined by the level of building society business and so are regarded as a simple function of the main two assets of mortgages and the liquid portfolio. The stock of mortgages is determined from its previous value by additions in the form of new advances and subtractions in the form of repayments. These repayments of mortgage principal, shown in the centre of the figure, are determined by two separate factors. First mortgages are repaid steadily under the terms of the original advance and hence repayments will be a function of the mortgages outstanding and the rate of interest. Monthly payments by most borrowers comprise an element of interest and element of repayment of principal. Since the size of these payments is often fixed, a rise in the interest element will tend to entail a fall in the repayment element. Second, mortgages may be repaid prematurely, often as the result of the desire to move house. This is shown as a function of the income of borrowers, the price of housing and the cost of borrowing.

Liquid assets on the other hand are affected in each time period by two rather different factors. First there is a need to maintain a satisfactory liquidity ratio and second liquid assets have an attraction in themselves as interest earners compared with mortgages. If the interest rates on liquid assets are relatively high societies may choose to hold more liquid assets now so that they can earn a higher rate of return and lend even more in the future. The net change in liquid assets, is therefore a function of the two competing rates of interest, the mortgage and market rates, and the inflow of new funds which can be used to buy the assets as well as being modified by existing liquidity and commitments to lend which will affect liquidity in the future. There was also a special government loan in 1974–75 made to societies at a favourable rate of interest to keep the mortgage interest rate down, and this is included specifically in the determination of the net change in liquid assets.

The building society sector is thus highly interrelated as can be seen from the number of endogenous variables among the determinants of assets on the righthand side of Figure 5.2. The only item left unexplained is the level of reserves and the consequent reserve ratio. For this return to the lefthand side of the figure. The net change in shares and deposits was explained when considering Figure 5.1, and this can be added to the previous stock to obtain the current stock of shares and deposits with building societies. As we have already estimated the asset side of the balance sheet we can calculate reserves as a residual. This completes the tour of the model.

Section 5.2 presents and justifies the precise specification of the model which is estimated and used in the analysis, simulations and forecasts in the rest of the book. The model used is set out in Table 5.1 and the definitions of variables are given in Section A.1 of the Technical Appendix.

5.2   The Specification and Estimation of the Model

The choice of the actual model to be estimated and the estimates to be used is not a simple one. There are three general factors which have to be taken into account in making a suitable choice: first the model must have a sound economic rationale; second, the findings must make full use of the experience of previous research work; and third, the statistical properties of the equations estimated must accord with the economic ideas and produce results which are of practical value.

The choice of particular functional forms and measures of variables is inevitably a compromise. Considerations of cost, practicality and the availability of data often mean that the ideal specification suggested by economic theory cannot be fully implemented. Our model is no exception to this, but hopefully the distortions involved are not of major importance. The first general simplification adopted, for example, is, with a couple of small exceptions, to use a linear form for the model. Nevertheless even this has resulted in substantial complications in the estimation owing to non-linear relations between equations, which necessitated the writing of special computer programmes to examine the behaviour of the model as a whole (see Technical Appendix, pp. 133–9). Experiments with other functional forms and the experience of previous research suggests that the assumption of linearity does not present any important drawback to understanding the working of the model.

The general procedure has been to build upon the most successful elements of previous research and to try to incorporate improvements in areas which were weaker. Thus this work is able to benefit from the experience which has already been gained in this field. Therefore the work of the following is considered in detail: Artis et al. (1975), Clayton et al. (1975), Foster (1975), Ghosh (1974), Hadjimatheou (1976), Hendry and Anderson (1976), HM Treasury (1977), London Graduate School of Business Studies (1976), Neuberger and Nichol (1976), O'Herlihy and Spencer (1972), Riley (1974) and Whitehead (1974). Of course, the blame for the final choice of model cannot be laid on their shoulders. None of these models replicates this book as they do not include sufficient of the period of the rapid rise in prices during the 1970s to explain it. Whatever the use which can be made of previous results it is clear, therefore, that a considerable amount of further estimation must be undertaken.

As is clear from Whitehead and Hadjimatheou, the last few periods of their studies after 1970 present problems in terms of the stability of parameters. Relations which have worked well during the 1950s and 1960s no longer act as good predictors in the 1970s. There are two possible reasons for this, either their original estimated specifications are not completely correct largely because their period of observation does not exhibit enough variance to cope with the more extreme values of the 1970s or because the actual structure of behaviour has changed. Estimation has therefore been approached from these two points of view. It has first been assumed that there is a single coherent structural form which can be applied to the entire estimation period between 1955 and 1976. Second it has been assumed that behaviour changed after 1970 and the model has been estimated with a structural shift at that point in all parameters. A further adjustment to this second approach has been tried by assuming that the period 1971—73 when the price explosion and other major fluctuations took place was affected by different factors, and hence the model should only be estimated with a structural shift for the period 1971—73. Clearly, only having further information up to 1976 makes the testing of this hypothesis rather weak.

Since the model is simultaneous most of the equations cannot be estimated independently without regard for each other. Second, since the variables are entirely time series, behaviour is highly correlated between time periods and the autoregressive structure of the model must be looked at carefully. This entails the use of a relatively complicated technique which takes account of both these factors. It uses instrumental variables to take account of the simultaneity and uses a maximum likelihood estimation of the equation taking the autoregression into account. This technique is well documented in econometric literature and gives the best estimates of the model we can obtain with the information and resources available. A full discussion of this method and its implications is given in the Technical Appendix (which is cross-referenced with the text), together with an exposition of all the other statistical problems encountered in the analysis.

Thus a choice has to be made not only between competing specifications of variables and functional forms but over the existence of structural change, simultaneity and autoregressive structure. This is no small task, which is further complicated by the existence of non-linear constraints between equations. A further aspect of the behaviour of the estimated model is therefore considered by running the entire model over the estimation period assuming that only predetermined and exogenous variables are known and leaving the model to generate the values of the endogenous variables. This gives two sorts of further information. First, it checks that the specification of the model is stable and that it behaves reasonably over the estimation period (in theory it is possible to examine the stability of the system directly from its reduced form, but that did not prove to be practicable in present circumstances). Second, the estimated time path of the endogenous variables can be examined to see if they follow the major characteristics of the actual values. A goodness-of-fit criterion such as the root mean square error (RMSE) does not indicate enough on its own. The model must exhibit the correct sorts of cyclical patterns, and also for example predict when interest rates change. It is worth mentioning this latter point at the outset although it is a very specific instance as it typifies the nature of the problems encountered. The savings rate is most closely explained by goodness-of-fit criteria with a strong auto-regressive structure, yet this structure entails that the discrete changes in the savings rate are almost invariably missed. A revised estimation procedure was therefore devised after examining the predicted values and the errors between them and the actual observed values.

The individual sections which follow, therefore, present the economic justification of our particular specification in the light of previous research and a statistical critique of the estimates obtaining taking account of all problems just mentioned. Although no individual equation is complete without the rest of the model the only sensible way to proceed is by taking each equation in turn. However, in order to keep the picture of the entire model in the reader's mind the complete system is set out in Table 5.1 and the estimated values of the parameters are given in Table 5.2.

The order in which equations are treated in a simultaneous model is somewhat irrelevant since the equations are interdependent, but to have some logic in the ordering the most interesting variable, house prices, will be taken first working on through the model by considering its endogenous determinants in turn.

Table 5.1. The estimated model

1. $PH = a_1 + a_2 PH_{-1} + a_3 YRA + a_4 IM + a_5 MA + a_6 HCO + a_7 HCP + a_8 PC + e_1$

2. $HCP = b_1 + \sum\limits_{i=2}^{9} b_i HSP_{2-i} + b_{10} IMD4 + \sum\limits_{i=11}^{13} b_i Q_{i-9} + b_{14} D3 + b_{15} D4 + e_2$

3. $HSP = c_1 + c_2 HSP_{-1} + c_3 MTR + c_4 BR_{-1} + c_5 PHCC + c_6 D3 + c_7 D4 + c_8 D8$
   $+ c_9 D9 + \sum\limits_{i=10}^{12} c_i Q_{i-8} + e_3$

4. $MA = d_1 + \sum\limits_{i=2}^{4} d_i MC_{2-i} + \sum\limits_{i=5}^{7} d_i Q_{i-3} + e_4$

5. $MC = f_1 + f_2 MC_{-1} + f_3 YRA + f_4 IM + f_5 SDD + f_6 LRBS_{-1} + f_7 RRD + f_8 PHPC$
   $+ \sum\limits_{i=9}^{11} f_i Q_{i-7} + e_5$

6. $MR = g_1 + g_2 MR_{-1} + g_3 AM_{-1} + g_4 IM + g_5 SDD + g_6 PHD + g_7 YA$
   $+ \sum\limits_{i=8}^{10} g_i Q_{i-6} + e_6$

7. $ALD = h_1 + h_2 LR_{-1} + h_3 IMBR + h_4 SDD + h_5 GL + h_6 D5 + \sum\limits_{i=7}^{9} h_i Q_{i-5} + e_7$

8. $AOL = j_1 + j_2 AOL_{-1} + j_3 ANOL_{-1} + e_8$

9. $SR = k_1 + k_2 SR_{-1} + k_3 YA + k_4 ISG + k_5 BR + k_6 D5 + \sum\limits_{i=7}^{9} k_i Q_{i-5} + e_9$

10. $SW = l_1 + l_2 SW_{-1} + l_3 YA + l_4 YT + l_5 IS + l_6 D5 + \sum\limits_{i=7}^{9} l_i Q_{i-5} + e_{10}$

11. $ICR = m_1 + m_2 SDS + m_3 ICR_{-1} + \sum\limits_{i=4}^{6} m_i QA_{i-2} + e_{11}$

12. $IS = n_1 + n_2 ITC + n_3 LR_{-1} + e_{12}$

13. $IM = p_1 + p_2 IM_{-1} + p_3 IS_{-1} + p_4 ISD + p_5 T + p_6 LR_{-1} + e_{13}$

14. $RR = q_1 + q_2 RR_{-1} + \sum\limits_{i=3}^{5} q_i Q_{i-1} + e_{14}$

15. $ME = r_1 + r_2 ME_{-1} + r_3 MA + r_4 YA + r_5 BR + r_6 PHPC + \sum\limits_{i=7}^{9} r_i Q_{i-5} + e_{15}$

16. $YRA = \sum\limits_{i=0}^{3} (Y/PC)_{-i}/4$

17. $IMD4 = (IM - IM_{-4})/IM_{-4}$
18. $MTR = MT/PH$
19. $MT = MA + ME$
20. $PHCC = PH/CC$
21. $HP = HP_{-1} + HCP + LAHS - SC$
22. $SDD = SR - SW + ICR$
23. $LRBS = (AL - MC)/ATOT$
24. $AL = AL_{-1} + ALD$
25. $ATOT = AM + AL + AO$
26. $AM = AM_{-1} + NA$
27. $NA = MA - MR$
28. $RRD = RR - R\hat{R}$
29. $RR = (ATOT - SD)/ATOT$
30. $SD = SD_{-1} + SDD$
31. $PHPC = PH/PC$
32. $YA = \sum_{i=0}^{3} Y_{-i}/4$
33. $ISG = IS/(1 - YT/100)$
34. $SDS = [(SD + SD_{-1})/2] [(IS + IS_{-1})/200]$
35. $QA_i = Q_i t \quad t \geqslant 45$
    $\quad\quad = 0 \quad\quad t < 45$
36. $PHD = (PH - PH_{-1})/PH_{-1}$
37. $LR = (AL/ATOT)100$
38. $ISD = IS - IS_{-1}$
39. $IMBR = IM - BR$
40. $AOL = \ln(AO)$
41. $ANOL = \ln(AL + AM)$
42. $ME = MAB + MAI + MALA$
43. $LRHA = (AL - OMC)/ATOT$
44. $OMC = OMC_{-1} + MC - MA$
45. $IS = IS^*$

$-i$ denotes a lag of i periods
$\char`\^$ denotes the estimated value

$IS^* = IS_{-1}$ if $|I\hat{S} - IS_{-1}| < 0.25$ or if $|I\hat{S}_{-1} - IS_{-2}| < 0.25$ or if
    sign $(I\hat{S} - IS_{-1}) \neq$ sign $(I\hat{S}_{-1} - IS_{-2})$
$\quad = IS_{-1} + 0.25s$ otherwise
where $s = (I\hat{S} - IS_{-1})/0.25$ to the nearest integer

Table 5.2   Estimated equations

1. $PH = 15.70 + 0.9781PH_{-1} + 1.177YRA - 7.397IM + 0.0274MA - 0.1197HCO^*$
   $\quad$ (8.02) (0.0265) $\quad$ (0.484) $\quad$ (2.541) $\quad$ (0.0071) $\quad$ (0.0668)
   $\quad - 0.4048HCP^* - 0.08993PC \quad$ s.e./μ = 0.023
   $\quad$ (0.1796) $\quad\quad$ (0.09779)

2. $HCP = 944.75 + [0.2793 + 0.1645L + 0.0833L^2 + 0.0359L^3 + 0.0219L^4 + 0.0417L^5$
   $\quad$ (4593) $\quad$ (0.0440) (0.0230) $\quad$ (0.0255) $\quad$ (0.0258) $\quad$ (0.0231) $\quad$ (0.0236)
   $\quad + 0.0951L^6]\ HSP - 3914IMD4 - 7455D3 - 6300D4 + 2106Q2 + 2348Q3$
   $\quad$ (0.0412) $\quad\quad$ (5278) $\quad$ (1901) $\quad$ (1897) $\quad$ (642) $\quad$ (723)
   $\quad + 5423Q4 \quad$ s.e./μ = 0.048 $\quad \rho = 0.75$
   $\quad$ (668)

3. $HSP = 22850 + 0.5033HSP_{-1} + 1844MTR - 2150BR_{-1} + 8381PHCC - 17560D3$
   $\quad$ (3262) (0.0641) $\quad\quad$ (655) $\quad$ (321) $\quad\quad$ (272) $\quad\quad$ (3764)
   $\quad + 15050D4 + 11510D8 - 8043D9 + 10880Q2 - 287.0Q3 - 2360Q4$
   $\quad$ (2640) $\quad\quad$ (3940) $\quad\quad$ (3714) $\quad$ (1193) $\quad\quad$ (1333) $\quad\quad$ (1238)
   $\quad$ s.e./μ = 0.076

4. $MA = - 3807 + [0.3756 + 0.4625L + 0.1862L^2]\,MC + 18.55Q2 + 54.89Q3 + 29.18Q4$
   $\quad$ (20.70) (0.0747) (0.1056) $\quad$ (0.0662) $\quad\quad$ (18.83) $\quad$ (18.79) $\quad$ (19.47)
   $\quad$ s.e. = 0.051

5. $MC = - 848.1 + 0.5816MC_{-1} + 7.164YRA - 132.6IM + 0.3828SDD + 6282LRBS_{-1}$
   $\quad$ (520.1) (0.1420) $\quad$ (17.350) $\quad\quad$ (45.4) $\quad$ (0.1250) $\quad$ (1890)
   $\quad + 6297RRD + 35.80PHPC + 61.97Q2 + 6.727Q3 - 96.81Q4 \quad$ s.e. = 0.092
   $\quad$ (1770) $\quad\quad$ (191.80) $\quad\quad$ (47.26) $\quad$ (52.650) $\quad$ (50.45)

6. $MR = 19.40 + 0.3957MR_{-1} + 0.007395AM_{-1} - 92251M + 0.1519SDD + 169.4PHD$
   $\quad$ (33.68) (0.0909) $\quad\quad$ (0.003805) $\quad\quad$ (7.037) $\quad$ (0.0236) $\quad\quad$ (77.8)
   $\quad + 0.007308YA + 23.24Q2 + 32.26Q3 + 22.11Q4 \quad$ s.e./μ = 0.076
   $\quad$ (0.004073) $\quad$ (4.98) $\quad\quad$ (4.38) $\quad\quad$ (4.65)

7. $ALD = 274.2 - 23.02LR_{-1} - 4.417IMBR + 0.4144SDD + 1.130GL - 281.0D5$
   $\quad$ (188.5) (12.52) $\quad\quad$ (15.030) $\quad\quad$ (0.0654) $\quad$ (0.179) $\quad$ (84.6)
   $\quad + 84.85Q2 + 71.64Q3 + 85.22Q4 \quad$ s.e./μ = 1.147 $\quad \rho = 0.1$
   $\quad$ (26.20) $\quad$ (24.69) $\quad$ (23.23)

8. $AOL = -0.1135 + 0.9774AOL_{-1} + 0.0279ANOL_{-1} \quad$ s.e./μ = 0.005 $\quad \rho = 0.35$
   $\quad$ (0.2054) (0.0330) $\quad\quad$ (0.0392)

9. $SR = -86.45 + 0.9671SR_{-1} + 0.009178YA + 45.53ISG - 26.59BR - 99.13D5$
   $\quad$ (69.10) (0.0783) $\quad\quad$ (0.017020) $\quad$ (21.98) $\quad$ (9.57) $\quad$ (77.51)
   $\quad -41.76Q2 - 55.92Q3 - 64.37Q4 \quad$ s.e./μ = 0.100
   $\quad$ (24.34) $\quad$ (24.11) $\quad$ (24.20)

10. $SW = -183.7 + 0.8574SW_{-1} + 0.0329YA + 6.600YT - 35.56IS + 264.5D5$
    $\quad$ (172.6) (0.0806) $\quad\quad$ (0.0089) $\quad$ (5.502) $\quad$ (21.52) $\quad$ (62.3)
    $\quad - 43.03Q2 - 21.14Q3 - 61.69Q4 \quad$ s.e./μ = 0.122
    $\quad$ (18.40) $\quad$ (18.29) $\quad$ (18.31)

$CR = -6.291 + 0.2602SDS - 0.6535ICR_{-1} - 0.2492Q2A - 0.3863Q3A + 0.3335Q4A$
     (1.337) (0.0136)   (0.0738)   (0.0736)   (0.0571)   (0.0744)

s.e./μ = 0.153

$S = 1.758 + 0.4382ITC - 0.04322LR_{-1}$ $R^2 = 0.947$ s.e./μ = 0.070   d.w. = 0.834
   (0.420) (0.0147)   (0.02801)

$M = 0.6075 + 0.3684IM_{-1} + 0.7791IS_{-1} + 0.3444ISD - 0.01071LR_{-1} + 0.02683T$
   (0.3748) (0.1041)   (0.1157)   (0.1303)   (0.02348)   (0.00955)

$R^2 = 0.988$ s.e./μ = 0.024   d.w. = 2.20

$RR = 0.001776 + 0.8567RR_{-1} + 0.01013Q2 + 0.01317Q3 + 0.00936Q4$
   (0.005104) (0.0692)   (0.00141)   (0.00142)   (0.00127)

s.e./μ = 0.064 ρ = 0.15

$ME = -7208 + 0.5974ME_{-1} - 0.07819MA + 0.01487YA - 10.51BR + 74.82PHPC$
   (2023) (0.1129)   (0.03630)   (0.00480)   (3.15)   (19.41)

   $+ 14.81Q2 + 25.87Q3 + 8.349Q4$ s.e./μ = 0.149
   (7.71)   (7.76)   (7.695)

quations 2 and 4 L^i is used as the lag operator for lags of length i for ease of exposition.
dard errors in parentheses.
otes multiplication by 10^4.

5.3   The Housing Market

5.3.1 House Prices

The general specification derived in Chapter 2 was:

$$PH = f_1(Y, MA, MO, IM, NP, t, HCP, PC, PHE, PCE, HP_{t-1}) \quad (1)$$

This can be estimated in several ways depending upon the choice of form for f_1 and the specification of the individual variables. Previous experience is not very helpful here as only Neuberger and Nichol, the London Business School and the Treasury estimate direct new house price functions and only the first of these is a reduced form equation in the same sense as equation (1). The Treasury model is specified in the form of an excess demand function where the change in house prices is a function of the mortgage rate of interest, adjusted for tax relief, new building society mortgage advances and investment expenditure on private dwellings with a complex lag structure. The London Business School on the other hand use a price relating equation augmented by building society advances by suggesting that new house prices depend upon the level of net new advances in real terms, the implicit deflator for fixed domestic capital formation and a time trend. Both of these two explanations put heavy direct emphasis on the rôle of building society advances on house prices. The result of this is, in the

Treasury case for example, that 'a sustained 10 per cent increase in gross advances over the 1974 level would, other things being equal, add £1,200 a year to house prices'. This is a striking conclusion and places a very substantial rôle on building society lending, which must be borne in mind when considering the results of the specification used here. Neuberger and Nichol on the other hand estimate versions of a general linear specification of the form:

$$PH_t = c_0 + c_1 IM + c_2 MA + c_3 Y + c_4 PC + c_5 PH_{t-1} \qquad (2)$$

and experiment by adjusting the mortgage rate of interest for tax relief and by adding a squared term in mortgage advances.

These equations and the linear structural demand equations of Hadjimatheou and Whitehead (although they also estimate on a per capita basis) suggest that a linear form for equation (1) would be appropriate. Nevertheless several different forms of equations were experimented with. There was little to choose between linearity and log-linearity and hence the latter was rejected as it would make the estimation of the simultaneous model more complex. Specifications in first differences and first differences of logarithms turned out surprisingly poorly. Surprisingly, because from the nature of time series analysis one would expect that slowly moving variables are often best explained in terms of levels while more rapidly moving variables are explained by first or even second differences. The linear specification was therefore preferred.

The specification of the individual variables proved rather difficult owing to the very obvious multicollinearity between many of the variables. Rather than resort to purely statistical methods (such as ridge regression or regression on the principle components) it is preferable to keep to the most important economic determinants so that the interpretation of the results should be clearer even if the estimates should prove to be slightly less efficient. This gave a specification of:

$$PH_t = \alpha_1 + \alpha_2 YRA_t + \alpha_3 IM_t + \alpha_4 MA_t + \alpha_5 HCO_t$$
$$+ \alpha_6 HCP_t + \alpha_7 PC_t + \alpha_8 PH_{t-1} + e_{1t} \qquad (3)$$

The main omissions from this equation are the stock of private housing in the previous period, population and the time trend. Of these only population as an indicator of household formation is at all worrying. Hadjimatheou and Whitehead both express demand on a *per capita* basis to avoid collinearity problems but equations of this form are not better determined than equation (3), collinearity actually leads to coefficients with perverse signs. Price expectations are incorporated by assuming naively that:

$$PHE_t = (1 + \lambda)PH_{t-1} . \tag{4}$$

PCE is rather more difficult to deal with since it is arguable that we might be more concerned with the rate of inflation than the level of prices, however, attempts to include this were not successful. Similarly trying PC_{t-1} by using the same argument as equation (4) did not prove fruitful, therefore, only the current price of alternative products is included. This treatment of expectations is not very attractive, and a more satisfactory justification for the inclusion of the lagged dependent variable is to take account of the failure of prices to adjust to their desired levels within each quarter. Especially under conditions of rapid changes some lagged adjustment is to be expected. Attempts to introduce local authority rents as a measure of the attractiveness of alternative housing were discarded but it was found that the use of all other completions, HCO, did give an indication of the effects of activity in the rest of the housing market, and it was therefore included as a proxy for this. The specification is completed by the two building society variables. Although originally it was hoped to include both mortgage lending by building societies and other institutions, other lending as a separate variable did not make a useful contribution and total lending was a poorer explanatory variable than building society lending alone. To some extent this can be explained by the existence of two opposite effects. On the one hand lending by other institutions is additional to building society lending in that other institutions may lend on other sorts of properties, thatched cottages, second homes, or be prepared to advance larger sums, while on the other hand they may be substitutes for building society lending. Thus building society lending may move in the same or the opposite direction as other lending depending upon the circumstances. A particular example of an offsetting movement occurred when funds available from local authorities were cut in 1974, building societies specifically earmarked sums for those categories of borrowers whose source of finance had been removed and were nominated to them by local authorities.

The estimates obtained (shown in Table 5.2) indicate that house prices are sensitive to changes in the main determining variables;

however it is not possible to say how sensitive without considering the model as a whole. The high value of the coefficient for lagged prices shows that long-run effects will be much greater than short-run effects. It also indicates that expectations are not fully taken into account (the incorporation of a simple autoregressive process, while insignificant, corrects this). The size of the coefficient also appears to suggest that a first difference structure might be more appropriate but the estimates from that model were less reliable in prediction. The individual coefficients are quite well determined and the overall level of explanation not surprisingly very high. A change in building society advances by 1 per cent in 1970 had the immediate effect of changing new house prices in the same direction by 0.11 per cent. In the longer run this rises to 0.58 per cent. Expressing this in money terms, if building societies had lent a further £100 million in the first quarter of 1970 this would have increased house prices by nearly £200 immediately and by nearly £1,000 in the long-run. The effect of mortgage lending on house prices is thus substantial but not as large as sometimes suggested.

There is some evidence to suggest that our specification is too sluggish in the short run and too responsive in the long run. Rather than concentrating on the extreme closeness of the determination of the equation (Table 5.2 shows that the remaining standard error is only 2.3 per cent of the mean price) it is more interesting to look at how the endogenous simulation performs. Starting in 1970 Figure 5.3 shows that predicted prices do not keep pace with actual prices during the period of the most rapid rise and that they overshoot when prices reached their temporary peak in 1974. The main errors occur when predicted prices cannot keep pace with the 17.5 and 9.0 per cent jumps in actual prices in the last two quarters of 1972 giving values some 10.5 and 10.7 per cent below the true ones. The worst error occurs in the second quarter of 1974, however, when prices are overpredicted by 16.7 per cent. There are two points which can be put in mitigation for this, firstly we have already predicted four complete years ahead with what is essentially a short-run model whose forecasts would normally be limited to nearer two years and second the fluctuations in the variables are at their extremes. In estimating any model from observed data responses to variation are averaged to some extent and hence the estimated response to extremes will always be an underestimate. The extreme is treated as being abnormal and that part of it is an unpredictable error.

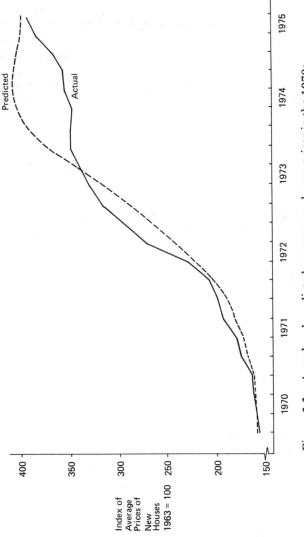

Figure 5.3   Actual and predicted average new house prices in the 1970s
(from the simulation of the model using known exogenous variables only)

House prices are also very responsive to the mortgage interest rate. Although in terms of 1970 values a change in the mortgage rate of 1 per cent only has an impact of 0.4 per cent on the level of house prices everything else being held constant, when the whole model is solved for a single period the effect is a change of 0.65 per cent. In the long run the effect is even more substantial. If the mortgage interest rate rises mortgage commitments fall and hence advances fall through liquidity rises helping to offset this slightly. Prices therefore fall (in relative terms) not only because of the rise in interest rates but also because of the decline in mortgage lending. After a year the change in interest rates begins to affect completions adversely, which helps to restrict the fall in prices.

A 1 per cent rise in real incomes results in a 0.62 per cent rise in house prices immediately at 1970 levels with a steady diminution in effect thereafter as the stimulus works its way through the system. Once again it is worth recalling the pattern of the model. A rise in incomes not only results in an increased demand for new houses and for mortgage advances but it also results in an increased flow of funds into building societies, hence permitting further lending. The model also suggests that not only is there an increased demand for housing but that there is an increased turnover as well.

The really interesting aspect, however, is not how income affects price but how it affects the demand for new housing. What is required is the solution of the model for private house completions in order to do this. However, first the determination of completions in the structure of the model should be considered.

5.3.2 House Completions

Of the three simultaneously determined endogenous variables in equation (3), IM, MA and HCP, the most appropriate choice for the next to be examined is HCP. Chapter 2 suggested that there was a straightforward distributed link between housing starts, HSP, and housing completions:

$$HCP_t = a\sum_i \lambda_i HSP_{t-i} \qquad (5)$$

The only concern is with the form of the lag. There is little to choose between varying specifications provided that due allowance is made for the very severe winter of 1963 and the introduction of the Betterment

Levy in 1967 (labelled D3 and D4 respectively in the model as shown in Table 5.1, equation 2). The former held down output and the latter pushed it up as people tried to avoid paying the tax by bringing construction forward.

It is to be expected that some disturbance to the form of the function in response to more immediate economic pressures would be observed. In particular if interest rates rose while houses were under construction this would tend to make some projects impossible to finance and completions would fall relative to previous starts. A short-run reaction to price might also be observed; if prices rose rapidly then there would be an extra incentive for builders to complete more quickly. Most houses are completed within two years of being started, the majority taking between three months and a year. Therefore, although no constraints were imposed on the lag distribution on starts initially, it is expected to fade out towards zero after six or eight quarters, as was also experienced by Whitehead and Hadjimatheou. In practice seven quarters seemed to be about right whether Almon or unconstrained lag distributions were used, thus suggesting a relation of the form:

$$HCP = \beta_1 + \sum_{i=2}^{9} \beta_i HSP_{t-i+2} + \beta_{10} IMD4 + \beta_{11} PHD4 + \beta_{12} D3$$
$$+ \beta_{13} D4 + \beta_{14} Q2 + \beta_{15} Q3 + \beta_{16} Q4 \tag{6}$$

where

$$IMD4_t = (IM_t - IM_{t-4})/IM_{t-4}$$

and

$$PHD4_t = (PH_t - PH_{t-4})/PH_{t-4}$$

The Qj's are seasonal constants.

The final estimated version shown in Table 5.1 with parameter values in Table 5.2 differs from this slightly because the price term was found to have a negative coefficient. The initial response to this was to try to find the reason as it might indicate a more general error of specification. The first suggestion stems from the analysis of Chapters 2 and 4 where it was shown that starts respond more quickly to price changes than do completions as they require a smaller use of resources

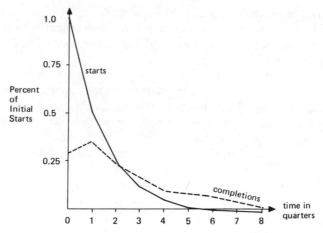

Figure 5.4   The response of private housing starts and completions
to a rise in housing starts of one per cent in 1970

by the builder. Thus under rapid price changes starts would move ahead more rapidly than completions and with the use of a single lag distribution would be shown up by a negative price coefficient. A second and less attractive explanation is of course that the supply and demand functions are being confused and a demand relation is being picked up. To some degree the use of simultaneous equations methods and the actual form of the specification should make this relatively unlikely. However, in any case, when the equation was rerun with the omission of price the determination was improved and the particular estimates using an Almon lag shown in Table 5.2 were adopted. (The lag operator L^i is used for notational convenience in the table.)

Chapter 2 noted there is a much heavier weight on recent periods than would be expected and a much lighter weight on two and three period lags. This same form was observed whatever estimation method was used and is independent of the particular third order polynomial used here. The explanation advanced was that the estimated relation shows the economic as well as the technical link between starts and completions. It is reassuring to note that when the model is run the initial change in starts has fed through completely onto completions after just over a year. The general time path of the two variables is shown in Figure 5.4.

5.3.3 Housing Starts

Having linked completions to starts the housing sector of the model can be completed by explaining the supply of starts. Chapter 2 presented a supply function for starts where they were determined by the availability of finance for housebuilding, the prevailing rate of interest on borrowing and the ratio of new house prices to construction costs. This is not a particularly contentious form of specification, Whitehead and Hadjimatheou both use versions of it. Whitehead specifically includes the building societies' financial position as a variable, and while she uses the inflow of funds we have used the total lending actually made available for house purchase. The inflow of funds has a contingent effect depending, as seen in Chapter 3, upon, among other variables, the liquidity and reserve positions of building societies. Secondly a partial adjustment mechanism is assumed in preference to Whitehead's variable lags. (Note that Hadjimatheou's model assumes there are no current determinants of starts.)

There are problems in choosing a cost series against which to relate house prices. The construction cost index itself (drawn from *Housing and Construction Statistics*) suffers from the drawback that it already includes an element of profit and hence understates the attractiveness of construction to builders. Constructing one's own index as Whitehead does is a way round this, but not necessarily a totally satisfactory one as it is difficult to choose suitable weights. In particular the use of constant weights will not take proper account of the striking variation in land prices during the 1970s discussed in the last chapter (pp. 52–5). Several different indices were tried with varying success and the final specification, which uses the published index, can only be described as an approximation:

$$HSP = \gamma_1 + \gamma_2 HSP_{-1} + \gamma_3 MTR + \gamma_4 BR_{-1} + \gamma_5 PHCC + \gamma_6 D3$$

$$+ \gamma_7 D4 + \gamma_8 D8 + \gamma_9 D9 + \text{seasonal constants} \qquad (7)$$

where PGDP is the GDP deflator and MALA is local authority mortgage lending. Unfortunately this equation is not very closely determined and shows strong positive first order autocorrelation.

Before leaving this subject note that it is possible to model the housing market in other ways, which also produce satisfactory results. The simplest of these is suggested by Neuberger and Nichol who model the whole market for new private housing by the supply and demand for completions. The supply of completions is dependent upon the lending for house purchase and the rate of interest with a partial adjustment mechanism. Their justification for this is very straightforward. In the very short run there can be no adjustment of the numbers of completions to changes in the price of new housing. Demand on the other hand will be highly elastic given the very small size of completions relative to the entire stock of existing housing. Although there are considerable attractions to this form of specification, the hypothesis about a short-run supply curve which is virtually vertical seems rather harsh and therefore a greater degree of flexibility and hence problems of simultaneity between demand and supply can be expected if they are specified in the form that Neuberger and Nichol suggest. Furthermore, a much better idea of the possible size of response that can be made over two periods if it is related to previous starts rather than just having a partial adjustment mechanism for completions themselves.

The Treasury model avoids any confusion over either starts or completions by concentrating on investment expenditures on housing. Investment is a function of personal disposable income, the mortgage interest rate net of tax, building society advances deflated by house prices to give an idea of the quantity of housing that can be financed and a time trend where there is a distributed lag on the coefficients. The price function is determined by the mortgage interest rate, building society advances and investment in private housing. (It is only really the complex lag structure which identifies this model.) Artis *et al.* pursue this sort of approach further by suggesting a disequilibrium model where the real price of housing changes in proportion to the excess demand gap for the stock of private housing. They incorporate this using a method suggested by Fair and Jaffee (1972) and used by Fair (1973) for the US housing market. This involves creating two disequilibrium variables, one for excess demand and one for excess supply. Thus with a single investment function the demand function is observed when there is excess supply and the supply function when there is excess demand, and the two sets of time periods can be separated out to enable estimation. Unfortunately the results prove unacceptable to the authors and the specification is rejected. The rest of their analysis rests on an equilibrium model which tries to establish the effects of building society rationing on housing investment with the conclusion that 'rationing rarely has important effects' (Artis *et al.* (1975), p. 54). As they also admit, however, they have severe specification problems and we have chosen to follow the advice of their discussant Byatt (1975, p. 62):

> The subject is very difficult, and it is easy to criticise, but I think the chances of succeeding by trying to put everything into a simple econometric model are very low. Instead I would like to see much more partial work on the components of the relevant money and real markets, leading to a model of the financial sector of the housing market, which could be linked to models of the behaviour of builders and the demand for accommodation.

Moving on to consider the estimates obtained for the chosen specification in the light of this discussion of possible alternatives, Table 5.2 shows that the results are very promising. The coefficients all have the expected signs (from Table 5.1, equation 3) $c_3 > 0$, $c_4 < 0$, $c_5 > 0$ and are significantly different from zero at the one per cent level. The overall determination of the equation is high and compares favourably with Hadjimatheou's results for example as the estimation period used here shows a higher variance in housing starts than his. Using this equation alone gives short and long run elasticities of 0.17 and 0.35 for the availability of finance 0.56 and 0.13 for the cost of finance and 0.27 and 0.55 for relative profitability in 1970. This makes starts seem relatively insensitive, but of course in practice a tightening of the availability of finance will tend to be accompanied by an increase in the cost of finance, so that the two variables taken together will have a far greater effect on housing starts.

This completes the housing side of the model and the question posed originally about the nature of the demand function for new private houses can now be answered. Taking elasticities measured at 1970 values with a five-year horizon a price elasticity of 2.48 and an income elasticity of 0.89 are observed. At first glance the income elasticity seems unreasonably low until one considers what has happened to housing completions since 1968. While (real) incomes have risen substantially completions have fallen. Hence even taking all the other variables into account it is not surprising that the income elasticity should only appear to be around unity. Shorter estimation periods putting more weight on the 1950s and 1960s as opposed to the 1970s give considerably higher values.

The housing market is completed by a simple identity linking the stock of housing to the pre-existing stock plus new additions less dwellings closed, equation (21) in Table 5.1, which leads on to the consideration of the link between the housing and building society sectors, which is clearest in the form of building society lending.

5.4   The Asset Structure of Building Societies

Chapter 3 established a view of the aims of building societies, but the aims do not determine any one particular model so a choice must be made. The explanation can be divided into three sections for ease of exposition: first, how building societies decide upon the structure of their asset holdings given the inflow of funds which they have available; second, how that inflow of funds is itself determined and thus complete the explanation of the items in the balance sheet shown in Table 3.2; third, how building societies determine interest rates, a major determinant of the flows of funds.

Beginning, therefore, with the explanation of the asset structure of building societies, this structure can clearly be seen in Table 3.2, namely that total assets (ATOT) are made up primarily of mortgage assets (AM) plus liquid assets (AL) and a small amount of other assets (AO). It is possible to estimate this stock either directly or by considering changes in it during each time period. The latter has been chosen largely because the stock of mortgages is mainly a fixed item from the point of view of the building societies but also because decisions are taken about the flows rather than the stocks and the previous research already mentioned indicates that this is the most fruitful line of approach. Thus in period t, $ATOT_{t-1}$, AM_{t-1}, AL_{t-1} are known but the net increase in mortgages (NA_t), the net movement in liquid assets (ALD_t) and in other assets (AOD_t) have to be established to calculate $ATOT_t$, AM_t, AL_t and AO_t.

5.4.1 New Mortgage Advances

When considering building societies' aims it was noted that the really important feature in the determination of lending was the decision to lend itself, in the form of a mortgage commitment. The actual new lending which occurs (MA_t) is purely the lagged take-up of previous offers, i.e. mortgage commitments, MC_t. Thus lending can be represented by a simple distributed lag on commitments (equation 4 in Table 5.1)

$$MA_t = \sum_i \lambda_i MC_{t-i} + \text{seasonal variation} \qquad (9)$$

Of course these commitments themselves now have to be explained. This is a departure from previous research which developed models to explain advances directly, either in terms of the net addition to the stock of mortgages outstanding or as gross new advances. As is clear in Table 5.2, equation (4), the bulk of mortgages move from the commitment to the advance within six months, with an average lag of about ten weeks.

5.4.2 Mortgage Commitments

In moving the burden to explanation away from mortgage advances and on to mortgage commitments this already places constraints on the type of model which can be estimated. A strict flow of funds approach or asset demand model of the form of Clayton et al. (1975) or Ghosh (1974) is no longer appropriate as we are dealing with what people wish to do with funds rather than with what the outcome of their wishes turns out to be.

The determination of the level of lending was the main feature of the discussions of the aims of societies, and the summary at the end of Chapter 3 suggested that societies try to maximize lending subject to the flow of funds and a number of constraints. The maximum supply without constraint would clearly be the demand, so a simple specification of the demand for mortgages would be a suitable first step — say that they are a function of personal disposable income, YRA (defined in equation (16), Table 5.1), the price of the mortgage (i.e. the mortgage rate of interest, IM) and the relative price of housing compared to consumer prices in general, PHPC. This demand is not, however, met because of the constraints, in particular because of the net inflow of funds, SDD. The remaining constraints will have differing effects. The desire for virtually riskless loans will tend to be an unvarying restriction, while the desire for a smooth rate of growth and the rigidity of interest rates will tend to introduce a lag structure into the model. In its simplest form this could be represented by a partial adjustment model. The liquidity and reserve ratios act as the remaining constraints, so that, for a given inflow of funds, if liquidity is already low the level of lending will have to be reduced and similarly for the reserve ratio; although the desired reserve ratio will tend to fall over time with the increasing size and concentration of societies, and hence the particular means of incorporating the constraint will have to take account of this. The operation of the constraints prevents societies from offering all the lending they would like and so they need to be entered as arguments into the equation.

$$MC = f_2(YRA, IM, PHPC, SDD, LR, RR) + \text{seasonal factors} \quad (10)$$

where f_2 incorporates some form of distributed lag.

All the models mentioned at the outset use a direct function to estimate mortgages of the form of equation (10), with various constraints incorporated. The simplest of these is Clayton et al. who regress the outflow of funds to mortgage lending on the inflow of funds from shares and deposits. The London Business School add interest rates and deflate both flows by house prices with a distributed lag on the inflow of funds term, thus assuming that income and the liquidity and reserve ratios have no effect. The Treasury model following Riley adds an income term and suggests a first differences in logarithms form with appropriate lag distributions for the variables. This explicitly assumes that any of the constraints caused by RR and LR will be caught up in the lag structure as the desired level of mortgages is a constant proportion of the level of shares and deposits. Riley shows quite clearly that in this specification the inclusion of a price term does not add to the explanation. Ghosh does not consider the demand side, but in allocating building society assets specifies a full range of interest rates for the main possible forms in which assets can be held and estimates the model subject to the global constraint of the required minimum liquidity and reserve ratios.

All these models therefore lack an important part of the structure. O'Herlihy and Spencer confirmed by Hendry and Anderson, incorporate more of the structure by including two dummy variables in their estimating equation reflecting periods of mild and severe mortgage rationing by building societies respectively. These two dummy variables are proxies for the effects of the flow of funds and the constraints of the reserve and liquidity ratios. Whitehead and Hadjimatheou demonstrate that it is preferable to use some or all of the variables themselves rather than their proxies, first because the original variables are continuous and second because they do not involve the need to make subjective judgements over the degree of rationing imposed during any particular time period. Perhaps the most interesting approach to the problem of reconciling building societies' objectives in estimation comes from Hendry and Anderson who specify the aim in the form of an objective function where losses are assumed to be quadratic. There are four parts to the objective function: first, a constant proportion of deposits should be relent as mortgages; second, the net demand for new mortgages should be met; third, achieving the required reserve ratio entails obtaining the appropriate surplus; and fourth, there is a reluctance to change either lending levels or interest rates. Unfortunately, no results have yet been published from this model although the authors hope to do so. The computational problems involved are to say the least, not particularly simple, so this sort of approach was rejected on the grounds of practicality, although the conditions required for minimizing the loss function are not far removed from some of our equations. Further hope for this approach can be obtained from the work of Hewitt and Thom (1977) who present a simplified version of this model for Northern Ireland. They have actually obtained estimates of their model which contains only two elements in the loss function and all variables refer to Northern Ireland. Their model gives a similar demand function for mortgage advances with the addition of a repayments term. Much of their specification is included in the estimating equation shown in Table 5.1, equation (5) and versions of it were unknowingly estimated during the development of the model.

As Chapter 3 (p. 37) noted, Hadjimatheou was able to incorporate the liquidity and reserve ratio constraints directly into his model by assuming that building societies had a constant desires level for the liquidity ratio of 16 per cent.

If liquidity rises above 16 per cent this is said to indicate that there is no constraint on the supply of mortgage advances and hence the function to be estimated is a pure demand function. Otherwise the shortfall of advances below demand which building societies desire is

$$\frac{1}{1-RR} \, SD_t (0.16 - LR_t) \; .$$

This constraint is incorporated in estimation by assuming that only a proportion of this shortfall is actually imposed, hence enabling Hadjimatheou to include a supply constraint variable in addition to the demand factors which has the value zero if the liquidity is 16 per cent or greater and

$$\frac{1}{1-RR} \, SD_t (0.16 - LR_t)$$

otherwise.

It is obviously desirable to try to incorporate the supply constraint imposed by shortages in liquidity, but as Chapter 3 showed there is no evidence that the liquidity ratio desired by building societies is constant. There are two ways of proceeding. One is to replace the constant 16 per cent by LR_t^*, the desired level in period t, and have a simple relation to explain LR_t^*. This could be done by estimating some trend value for LR and assuming this was a proxy for LR*. The second is to approach the problem rather more indirectly and specify an explicit demand function for liquid assets by building societies, and it is this we have chosen to do. The variable wanted for inclusion in equation (19), Table 5.1, is the degree of constraint on lending imposed by any particular liquidity ratio, which is expected to be greater the lower is liquidity compared with outstanding commitments.

The particular form of the variable is difficult to specify but we have chosen to try the specification suggested by Norman Griggs (see p. 40), the Secretary-General of the Building Societies Association, that the liquidity ratio used by building societies for the purpose of assessing lending ability is after subtraction of mortgage commitments:

$$LRBS = \frac{(AL - MC)}{ATOT}. \tag{11}$$

An alternative specification on an end year basis was tried:

$$LRHA = \frac{(AL - OMC)}{ATOT} \tag{12}$$

where OMC is the level of commitments outstanding at the end of each quarter but this appeared in practice to be a weaker explanatory variable than LRBS. A linear specification was chosen rather than say a quadratic or assymmetric one for two reasons: first, as indicated, there is a moving trend round which to base the quadratic or assymmetry; and second, because building societies are not expected to become increasingly more generous with higher liquidity, there will be a limit to this. In the same way in the face of lack of liquidity we expect there to be limits to meanness, given the level of the inflow of funds. These two variables LRBS and SDD will work together and between them will pick up the constraint that liquidity imposes on lending.

The reserve ratio constraint is more difficult to deal with since, as was noted, the required, and hence it is likely the desired, ratio falls with increasing size of societies. It is not practicable to get a measure of the effect of the change in the size distribution of societies on the required reserve ratio and the first procedure suggested for the liquidity ratio has been adopted, namely that the required and desired liquidity ratios can be represented by a simple trend, estimated as equation (14) in Table 5.1.

The estimates shown in Table 5.2, equation (5), fit in with our preconceptions, but are perhaps not quite as well determined as would be ideal. The net inflow of deposits, liquidity and reserve variables work very well with satisfactory signs and magnitudes. The interest rate variable on the other hand suggests a fairly high degree of sensitivity if this equation is taken on its own with an elasticity of 2.32 at 1970 values. The income coefficient is not significantly different from zero and gives an elasticity of 0.95 which is lower than expected. This equation showed signs of multicollinearity as explained in more detail in the Technical Appendix and other specifications tended to compound rather than remove it; the explanatory value of the individual coefficients is therefore reduced. The equation forecasts satisfactorily and hence it was accepted.

5.4.3 Mortgage Repayments

In order to complete the model and obtain estimates of liquidity ratios for building societies it is not an estimate of mortgage advances that is required but of the stock of mortgages and the stock of liquid assets. To estimate mortgages outstanding therefore repayments of principal need to be subtracted from the sum of the previous stock and the current additions to it.

Mortgage repayments (MR) occur for two main reasons. First, as a part of the standard form of mortgage agreement whereby a fraction of the mortgage is repaid each month by the borrower, and second where the entire sum outstanding is repaid prematurely. Most premature repayments occur because the mortgagor wishes to move house and has to sell his existing house and terminate the mortgage on that property before he can take out a new mortgage to buy the new property. There are, however, also many premature repayments of mortgages by people who continue to live in the house on which the mortgage was secured. According to the Housing Policy Review Technical Volume part I (Cmnd 6851, 1977) the number of people involved is substantial, contrary to popular belief many people are keen to divest themselves of their mortgage debts at an early opportunity.

These latter repayments will be a function of the stock of mortgages outstanding, and the ability to repay largely in terms of incomes and related factors. However, it will also tend to be the case that the ability to move up the housing market and the ability to repay will be influenced by similar factors. Repayments, therefore, can be approximated as a function of the size of the existing stock of mortgages and the rate of turnover of house sales.

The standard mortgage is repayable in equal monthly instalments over 20 to 25 years. However, each payment is composed of a repayment of the principal and an interest payment on the sum outstanding. Thus when mortgages are new most of the monthly payment is composed of interest and the repayment element is small while the reverse is true when most of the loan has been repaid. For a particular mortgage MA* the size of the monthly payment for a term of m months is:

$$\frac{MA^*(1 + IM^*)^m IM^*}{(1 + IM^*)^m - 1}$$

where $IM^* = IM/100$. Of this monthly payment the amount of principal repaid is:

$$\frac{MA^*(1 + IM^*)^{j-1} IM^*}{(1 + IM^*)^m - 1}$$

in any particular month j. (See Riley (1974, p. 20) for a clear explanation of this.) Standard repayments vary over the time of the mortgage in some cases when interest rates change. The borrower is offered the option to keep his monthly payments to the society the same or to adjust his payments to the new rate of interest. Thus if interest rates rise some borrowers will elect to keep their monthly payments the same and hence the repayment of principal clement in the monthly payment will fall and the interest component rise, thus lengthening the term of the mortgage. This would lead to the expectation of a fall in repayments with a rise in interest rates. Obviously this will be correlated with the relation between new advances and repayments as *ceteris paribus* a higher rate of interest will mean a lower demand for new mortgages.

O'Herlihy and Spencer suggest a simple form of explanation to incorporate the two determinants of repayments where the repayments on existing mortgages are a simple geometric function of previous mortgage advances, a specification which is maintained by Hendry and Anderson with a more complex lag structure. The alternative approach, given that the mortgage advance explanation is not in net terms as the London Business School suggest, is to specify the determinants of the size of early repayments of mortgages directly. The most important reason for doing this as Riley makes clear is that there is no causal link between repayments and new advances, they are merely both part of the same transactions. In fact were it not for the specific concern with the demand for just a section of the housing market, it would be very tempting to follow the London Business School approach. Riley's equation has been adopted identically by the Treasury model (it is surprising they did not feel it necessary to re-estimate given the availability of a further five years of data) and it uses as its determinants of moving house, house prices, the flow of funds into building societies and the mortgage rate of interest. This is expressed in difference form on the grounds that repayments tend to bear a constant ratio to the outstanding stock of mortgages.

Hadjimatheou treats this slightly differently by suggesting that what the borrower is choosing is the structure of his portfolio rather than changing house, hence he introduces the general rate of return on other assets, proxied by minimum lending rate, into his equation as well as the mortgage rate of interest. The decision on the size of the debt is also affected by income and the rate of change of prices (although this latter is excluded from the final estimates). Equation (6) in Table 5.1 is of the same form with the addition of the flow of funds into building societies and the exclusion of the proxy for other rates of interest. This gives a plausible set of estimates as can be seen from Table 5.2, equation (6). The level of existing mortgages is the major determinant and the remaining variables explain the variation round this path. The simulation path is also well determined with the exception of slight overestimation in the middle of the period due to the over-prediction of the inflow of funds and hence lending which is explained in Section 5.5.

Having determined both the level of mortgage advances and the level of repayments the stock of mortgages outstanding, AM, can be obtained from:

$$AM_t = AM_{t-1} + MA_t - MR_t = AM_{t-1} + NA_t \qquad (13)$$

as is shown in Table 5.1 equations (26) and (27).

5.4.4 Liquidity

To complete the system the remainder of the building societies' balance sheet is required. So far only the size of mortgage assets is known, yet the liquidity ratio is an explanatory variable. Therefore either the level of liquid assets or the liquidity ratio itself must be explained. Explaining a ratio is very difficult unless it can be done by using a fixed relation in the sort of way that Hadjimatheou does. Unfortunately since it was argued that this fixed relation does not exist this course is not open. Chapter 3 argued that building societies had two motives for holding liquid assets: first the required minimum plus a precautionary surplus and second the attractiveness of liquid as opposed to mortgage assets for earning interest. Only Clayton et al. and Ghosh estimate an explicit function to explain the size of liquid assets and they disaggregate between different assets. The basic form of their relation is that the size of liquid assets depends upon relative interest rates. In the flow of funds approach used by Clayton et al. the major determinant of the change in any one asset is the inflow of funds to building societies. Our particular specification is a form of this approach and is shown as equation (7) in Table 5.1.

This in itself does not give the liquidity ratio as there is a further type of asset which has not yet been considered, which is largely composed of the societies' own offices and the land on which they stand. These assets form not only a very small proportion of the total, just over 1 per cent, but also a stable proportion. It will therefore simply be assumed that these bear a close relation to the level of business undertaken by societies (equation (8) in Table 5.1). As can be seen from equation (8), Table 5.2, a logarithmic specification gives an extremely closely determined relation where the standard error is only one half of one per cent of the mean stock of other assets.

Unfortunately the same cannot be said of the determination of the net change in liquid assets, however, this variable does present rather more extreme problems than do many others. It is a first difference and so is not readily explained by previous values, it fluctuates very widely with a coefficient of variation of 2.24 and a range from $-$£309 million to £607 million. Taking the period 1973—74, for example, the successive values of £ million are -256, 369, 128, 168, -309, 537, 607, 216. The liquidity ratio on the other hand is a ratio of two levels, not first differences, so it is much more stably determined with a root mean square error of only 1.31 per cent. Thus, turning to Table 5.1, equation (25), the asset side of the balance sheet is completed and it is possible to determine both the liquidity ratio itself, equation (37), and the ratio used in building society decision-making for the level of commitments from equation (23).

5.5   The Inflow of Funds to Building Societies

Having completed the asset side of the balance sheet the next step is to move on to consider the liabilities. In summarizing the aims of societies it was noted that the inflow of funds is the most important factor determining the volume of new lending. It is therefore essential to formulate a close specification of its determinants. The basic form of any such relationship would be that savings deposited with building societies are a function of the savings available for deposit and the rates of interest offered by building societies and by other competing uses of these funds. Not surprisingly there is no complete agreement between previous writers over the most suitable form for the explanation. However, three main possibilities exist: first explain the total stock of shares and deposits in any one time period, as is suggested by Ghosh and Parkin (1972); second use a flow approach determining the change in shares and deposits in each time period as do Clayton *et al.* (1975), the London Graduate School of Business Studies model (1976) and Hadjimatheou (1976); or third explain the components of this flow of funds separately as do O'Herlihy and Spencer (1972). Fortunately, much of the discussion over the most appropriate specification to use is eased by a very thorough examination of the relative merits of different forms in Foster (1975).

The general specification suggested is that the demand for building society shares and deposits (SD) is a function of the total ability to save which could be represented by some measure of wealth, or at any rate the wealth which could readily be converted into that form (CW) and of the attractiveness of the various assets including cash which could be held as alternatives. Attractiveness, is to quite a large extent a function of interest rates, where differentials will help to explain varying degrees of liquidity and risk. The rate of inflation or people's expectation of it might also be included to give an estimate of the cost of holding cash. Foster (1975) gives a very clear exposition of the merits of different specifications of this function for estimation and concludes that the optimal form is to explain the proportionate change in shares and deposits by the rate of interest on building society shares and deposits, the clearing banks deposit rate, the Trustee Savings Banks rate of interest, the change in the expected rate of inflation, real personal disposable income and a dummy variable to allow for the effects of the large tax cuts of 1972.

Chapter 3 distinguished between two major groups of savers who responded differently to various rates of interest. Crudely speaking this was the distinction between large and small savers, the latter of whom Foster describes as 'precautionary' savers whose interest elasticity of demand is low. Further it was noted that the interest rate sensitivity of savers was also affected by whether the saver was a non-taxpayer, a taxpayer at the standard rate, or a taxpayer at higher rates. The particular competing interest rates chosen are obviously only some of those which could possibly be included others being the Post Office investment account rate and the rates for loans to local authorities. The change in shares and deposits with building societies would be expected to increase inversely with competing interest rates and directly with the interest rates offered by the societies themselves. However, in so far as depositors hold funds with a building society as a means of aiding the obtaining of a mortgage from that society in the future, the rôle of interest rates becomes a little contradictory. The demand for deposits from this source will vary inversely with the mortgage rate of interest as the higher the rate of interest the lower the demand for mortgages. Hence since the main determinant of the mortgage rate is the rate of interest on shares and deposits, this gives a negative relationship between shares and deposits and their rate of interest which will tend to push any resulting coefficient which is estimated for their relation towards zero.

The main problem in completing the specification of the demand for building society deposits is the incorporation of the wealth variable. A direct linear specification would entail that the wealth element became increasingly important as wealth rises. This can be overcome by assuming that the relation is multiplicative rather than additive, but it is more usual to suggest that a change of a given number of percentage points in a rate of interest has the same proportionate effect on deposits whatever the level of interest rates. This would entail a semi-logarithmic specification, and one would normally wish to incorporate a partial adjustment mechanism into the model as three months is likely to be too short a period for holdings of financial assets to be able to adjust completely to their desired levels in the face of interest changes. The change in shares and deposits between periods is composed partly of the allocation of new wealth acquired in period t to particular assets and partly of the readjustment of holdings of pre-existing wealth. Foster effectively neglects the second change and concentrates on the first. This makes the task much easier as he no longer needs to measure convertible wealth, but merely additions to it which Foster proxies by real disposable income in period t. Disposable income is certainly a relevant variable from the point of view of the precautionary demand for deposits. If a constant income elasticity of demand is assumed the specification suggested by Foster is obtained.

However, it is possible to distinguish between the flow of funds into building societies, receipts (SR), and the outflow of funds, withdrawals (SW) (see p. 75). This separation has been made for two reasons, first because the work of O'Herlihy and Spencer (1972) and Hendry and Anderson (1976) suggests that the behaviour of receipts and withdrawals is not symmetric with respect to the determining variables and second because empirical work shows that the changes in the level of deposits can be determined rather more closely by making this distinction. O'Herlihy and Spencer observe substantially different coefficients in the two equations after taking signs into account. Hendry and Anderson give a more complex reform of the same specification, but this and the one shown in equations (9) and (10) in Table 5.1 are all the same model with minor differences reflecting different data periods and estimation methods. The main further difference is the explicit incorporation of the standard rate of income tax into the equations.

Of the other models which all deal with the change in shares and deposits directly, Hadjimatheou has an identical specification while the Treasury model grosses up the building society interest rate for taxation, drops the independent tax term and substitutes the local authority three month loan rate for minimum lending rate and the London Graduate School of Business Studies, Riley and Foster all have different functional forms. The London Graduate School of Business Studies uses a logarithmic specification with real disposable income, the yield on 2½ per cent consols, minimum lending rate and the grosses up savings rate, while Riley has a first difference version of the Treasury model with both deposits and income in logarithms. Presumably since the Treasury model leans heavily on Riley's work they feel that their specification is an improvement on his. The use of real values and non-linear specifications presents considerable problems for the simul-

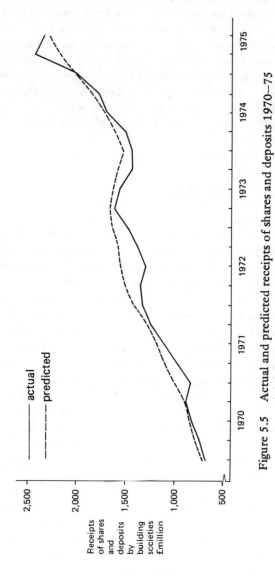

Figure 5.5   Actual and predicted receipts of shares and deposits 1970—75
(Simulation with actual values of exogenous variables only)

taneous estimation of the model (see Technical Appendix, p. 139) but this should not in itself dissuade anyone from using them. The particular relations have been chosen because, within the general framework, they give the most satisfactory estimates.

Taking the receipts equation first the estimates shown in Table 5.2 indicate that deposits increased steadily with income but are sensitive to changes in interest rates. The variable D5 is included to take account of the special effects of the three-day week in the first quarter of 1974 when building society receipts and withdrawals in common with other liquid forms of savings were heavily affected as people maintained consumption patterns despite the temporary shortfall in incomes. The simulation of the model over six years using actual values of the exogenous variables and solving for the endogenous values shows that despite the highly autoregressive nature of the relation it predicts well although overpredicting the inflow of receipts during 1972 and 1973 as is shown in Figure 5.5. This overprediction has implications for the whole model, since it leads to higher mortgage lending, and hence higher prices and output than would otherwise have been the case. Given the short-run nature of the model the performance of this simulation is very satisfactory. The maximum in the second quarter of 1973 is predicted correctly.

The equation for withdrawals is rather better determined although different in character. Withdrawals respond more strongly to changes in income reflecting the transactions demand for building society deposits. Competing rates of interest appeared to have no significant effect on withdrawals, the rate of interest offered to savers alone being a determining factor. It is interesting to note that the tax variable has the opposite sign to that expected and yet is a robust estimator to changes in the specification. It is noticeable that withdrawals were affected far more strongly than receipts by the three-day week.

Distinguishing withdrawals and receipts does not in fact complete the system because deposits also change as the result of interest payment. Most interest payments by building societies are not paid out to depositors but credited to their accounts, usually on a six-monthly basis. Hence:

$$\text{SDD}_t = \text{SD}_t - \text{SD}_{t-1} = \text{SR}_t - \text{SW}_t + \text{ICR}_t \tag{14}$$

where ICR is the interest credited to accounts. Fortunately calculating the value of this interest does not present any great problem as it is the value of the deposits multiplied by their rate of interest:

$$ICR = SD \times IS \tag{15}$$

In practice the estimation of equation (15) must be an approximation as there is more than one interest rate, the exact size of deposits on which the interest is calculated is not known, only the beginning and end period aggregate values, and the societies are paying out interest discontinuously at six-monthly intervals scattered non-randomly throughout the year thus the actual specification must be in the looser form of:

$$ICR_t = f \left(\sum_{i=0}^{2} w_i SD_{t-i} IS_{t-i} \right) + \text{seasonal factors} \tag{16}$$

where w_i is a weight, $\Sigma w_i = 1$.

The seasonal fluctuations are affected by two influences. First at low levels of interest credited they are less than the rounding error in the variable and hence cannot be included and second at higher levels of interest payments they increase with the average size of payment. Since there is no model to explain the nature of these fluctuations, the best determined empirical specification was chosen. The deposits on which interest is earned are those outstanding during the six months prior to payment and interest payable also varies with the rate of interest payable over the period. The seasonal constants are measured with a trend from the point they can be distinguished from the rounding errors. The equations are set out as (11), (34) and (35) in Table 5.1. Although the resulting estimates, shown as equation (11) in Table 5.2, are not so well determined as most other equations with a standard error to mean ratio of 15.3 per cent the magnitude of the errors is small compared with receipts less withdrawals and so the overall effect is not important.

It is not a simple matter to complete the liabilities side of the account as shown in Table 3.2. Official government loans can be treated as an exogenous factor as they were only available in 1974–75 as a specific arrangement to hold down interest rates. Reserves have followed a very stable path as shown in the discussion of the reserve ratio and can hence be estimated closely from the declining time path of the reserve ratio (equation (14) in Tables 5.1 and 5.2). The remaining items of accrued interest and other liabilities are trivial and can be estimated together as a residual (equation (29) in Table 5.1) since the level of total assets and hence total liabilities has been determined in the previous section and all other liabilities have now been covered in this section.

This now completes the explanation of the components of the balance sheet but one major aspect of building society behaviour is still not covered, namely the determination of interest rates.

5.6   Interest Rates

The interest rate structure of building societies is very straightforward. The rate offered to savers competes with interest rates offered by other institutions and is hence related to them. The degree of competitive margin required will depend upon the inflow of funds relative to commitments for mortgage lending and the existing liquidity position. The rate to mortgage borrowers will depend largely upon the maintenance of the margin of surplus over the savings rate including provision for taxation at the agreed composite rate. Hence with some flexibility for the liquidity position this gives a simple related specification. There is one proviso in that there is a general reluctance to change rates, hence in the short run a change in the competitive position will tend to be absorbed by accepting a change in liquidity and then the eventual interest change if required will tend to be 0.25 per cent or a multiple thereof (this practice ceased to be true in 1976 when a rate of 7.8 per cent was set).

All the cited models follow this pattern with minor modifications. Riley uses the ratio of mortgages to deposits to obtain a proxy for liquidity as do the London Business School and Hendry and Anderson following O'Herlihy and Spencer use both liquidity and reserve ratios which have a progressive effect the further they are from their mean. Thus if a ratio is relatively low the constructed variable becomes highly negative and conversely if it is relatively high. There is not much to choose between relative specifications and those (shown in Table 5.1, equations (12) and (13) and estimated in Table 5.2) appear to give both stable parameters and a reasonable representation of the underlying economic theory. It was originally anticipated that use of a relation of the form that O'Herlihy and Spencer suggest would give substantial improvements, but this did not turn out to be the case.

The major difference between the chosen estimation of interest rates and that of previous work lies in the way both the reluctance of societies to change their rates and the fact that rates were normally changed

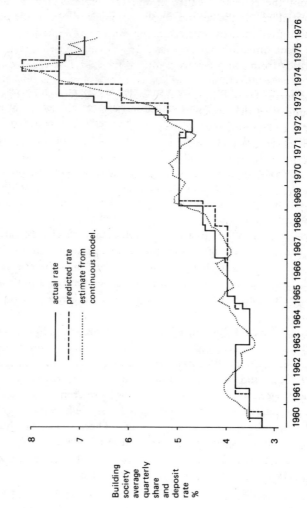

Figure 5.6   Actual and estimated interest rates offered to depositors

Building society average quarterly share and deposit rate %

actual rate
predicted rate
estimate from continuous model.

1960 1961 1962 1963 1964 1965 1966 1967 1968 1969 1970 1971 1972 1973 1974 1975 1976

in multiples of 0.25 per cent during the observation period have been incorporated. This was done by the following three stage procedure. First, equation (12) in Table 5.1 is estimated and values of IS are calculated from the estimated equation and the actual values of the explanatory variables. At the second stage, no change in IS is predicted unless the value predicted by our estimated version of equation (12) differs in the same direction but at least 0.25 per cent in two consecutive time periods from the previous predicted level. If a divergence of more than 0.25 per cent is observed in two consecutive periods then the third stage estimates the resulting change as the calculated value of IS from (12) rounded to the nearest 0.25 per cent as set out in equation (45) in Table 5.1. The estimates achieved by this procedure are shown in Figure 5.6 where the continuous line is the actual rate set by the building societies, the dotted line is the original estimated rate obtained from equation (12) and the dashed line shows the final estimate allowing for the reluctance to change and restricting changes to multiples of 0.25 per cent.

Note how the actual and predicted rates vary. There is a slight discrepancy in 1967—69 but the major difference occurs with the dramatic rise in interest rates in 1973 and 1974. Predicted rates rise more slowly than those that actually occurred, which suggests either that building societies reacted more quickly during this period to changes in the determining variables, or alternatively that they over-reacted. It also appears that later on in 1974 and 1975 that the societies did respond to the heavy pressure placed on them by the government to keep interest rates down, even allowing for the loan made to them during that period whose effect is incorporated through the liquidity variable. The divergence between the actual and predicted values is slightly aided by the assumption of a fixed three-month decision lag which does not vary with the size of the decision to be made. However, even if it is assumed that decisions are made immediately during the 1970s the general pattern of the divergence between actual and predicted interest rates is not altered, and attempts to estimate a variable decision lag were not sufficiently successful to be incorporated.

The root mean square error of the three-stage procedure is 0.35 per cent which when divided by the mean interest rate gives a ratio of 0.008 compared with the first stage result of 0.070, although of course these are not the same statistic. (This is not quite a fair comparison as an autoregressive specification would have given a ratio of 0.044, but this resulted in a failure to predict changes in the rate.) This specification of the savings rate is highly satisfactory, but it cannot be applied to the mortgage rate, first, because the change in the rate is a gradual process — it is applied to new borrowers immediately and to existing borrowers when they can be informed and put the matter in hand — and second because societies charge a range of interest rates on mortgages and the observed rate is only an average.

The share rate to savers is usually expressed net of tax, whereas the margin between the share and mortgage rates for societies must be calculated after tax. Hence the composite rate of tax paid by building societies (T) must be included in the explanation of the mortgage rate. Thus incorporating this and the fact that mortgage rates will tend to follow changes in the share rate (ISD) allowing for the building societies liquidity position after taking their commitments into account, LRBS = (AL − MC)/ATOT, equation (13) in Table 5.1 is obtained.

This completes the building society section of the model with the various identities shown in Table 5.1. There is one further stochastic equation to be estimated since not all lending is undertaken by building societies.

5.7   Lending by Other Institutions

The other models examined do not include lending by other institutions, with the exception of the London Business School who include loans for house purchase by local authorities. Even so they include it as an exogenous variable. The main other lending institutions besides local authorities are banks and insurance companies. These three separate items have been taken together, although it is clear that their time paths are by no means the same, largely for reasons of simplicity and convenience, but also because they will offset each other to some extent. In particular they are subject to the same sorts of demand factors. On the whole the terms of building society mortgages are preferable to those advanced by other institutions (with the exception of some local authority mortgages and loans to employees by financial institutions). These loans, therefore, will be more attractive the harder it is to get building society mortgages. Thus other lending will vary inversely with building society lending. In addition demand will vary with income, the cost of borrowing (the rate of interest) and the relative attractiveness of house ownership compared with other assets as indicated by its relative price. The estimated equation is thus as is shown in Tables 5.1 and 5.2 equation (15) where ME is lending by other institutions, namely by banks (MAB), by local authorities (MALA) and by insurance companies (MAI), giving $ME \equiv MAB + MALA + MAI$.

The estimates given in Table 5.2 conform to expectations about signs and magnitude. The income elasticity of demand is 1.06 in the short run and 2.64 in the long run at the mean (the 1970 value is abnormally low), while the interest rate elasticities are 0.62 and 1.54 in the short and long run respectively. The drawback of this specification is that it assumes that the only constraint on borrowing is the rate of interest. Clearly other supply contraints are imposed in practice, but it would require specific explanations for the individual institutions to do this, and this is not worthwhile in the present context. The interest rate therefore has to act as a proxy for all supply constraints.

This completes the exposition of the detailed estimates of the model and an answer can now be provided to the prime question of our book — what effects does building society behaviour have upon house prices?

6 The Effects of Building Society Behaviour on House Prices

6.1 The General Picture

The general nature of the effects of the actions of building societies on house prices should be clear from Chapter 5. None of these effects are startlingly new, but it is now possible to assess the numerical magnitude of any particular action. Building societies have three main variables they can affect directly which will in turn affect house prices: mortgage commitments and hence mortgage advances; the rate of interest charged on mortgages; and the rate of interest offered to savers. They can also alter their demand for liquid assets but this is not such an immediately relevant variable. The particular influences are straightforward and can be expressed in terms of 1970 values: (1) a 1 per cent rise in mortgage advances raises house prices by 0.58 per cent in the long run; (2) a 1 per cent fall in the mortgage rate of interest causes house prices to rise by 0.65 per cent immediately (a more sensitive effect than (1)); (3) a 1 per cent fall in the savings rate causes a 0.2 per cent rise in house prices (the mortgage rate of interest changes as a consequence and has more effect in the short run than the decrease in the inflow of funds). All these changes assume that the exogenous variables remain at their actual values but that the endogenous variables in the model can all change.

From these influences it can be concluded that had building societies decided to lend less on mortgages or put up the mortgage rate of interest they could have lessened the rate of inflation in house prices during the 1970s. Putting up the savings rate is of course a double-edged weapon as it both raises the mortgage rate of interest and the inflow of money into societies and hence with constant parameters would lead to an increase in lending. In these findings the interest effect is stronger than the lending effect. These conclusions are of course neither novel nor particularly illuminating. The question at issue is not can building societies raise house prices, because the answer is obviously yes, but how much did they do so during the early 1970s and did this represent any change in their activities.

The first point to note is that building society behaviour cannot be treated alone. All the variables in the system did change during the period 1971—74 and can be expected to continue to change. Thus while building society activity may be raising house prices, other activity such as housebuilding may be pushing them down and the result will be stable prices. Under these circumstances one would argue that building society activity did not increase house prices it merely stopped them falling. The model could be run over the 1970s and solved for the values of, say, building society lending which would have kept house prices constant. This would give a ludicrous set of results by 1974 with building society lending trying to offset the effects of increased incomes and construction costs. A more useful alternative perhaps would be to re-run the model to see what lending would have been required to keep the rise in house prices in line with the general rate of inflation. Nevertheless this still assumes that the policy being considered is one of trying to offset other influences. Chapter 5 posed the problem of trying to decide whether behaviour during the 1970s was consistent with that during the previous fifteen years, or whether structural changes occurred. Building society behaviour did not result in rapid or widely criticized rises in house prices during the 1950s and 1960s, hence if their behaviour continued on the same basis during the 1970s, this evidence might be used towards its not having had an appreciable effect during the 1970s. This, however, is not sufficient evidence on its own because it may merely be that building societies' behaviour is inflationary under extreme values of the determining variables.

Taking the problem of consistent behaviour first, this can be decided by seeing whether the parameters of the model change when the 1970s are also incorporated in the estimation. The methods used are set out in the Technical Appendix, but the results are fairly clear. Trying to assume that the whole period from 1971 onwards is subject to a consistent structural change is not very productive. Although the hypothesis is sustained in some cases it is not in general a clear representation of the changes. The main effect is that any parameters directly related to either house prices or consumer prices behave differently. Thus people react differently to substantial price inflation from the mild inflation experienced previously. In particular, relative prices and rates of change of prices are much less important outside the 1970s, reflecting two factors, first, if there is not much change in a variable people tend to find it less important and second if there is less variation in a variable it is more difficult to observe its effect. This is revealed by coefficients with values nearer zero but with increased variances.

The second and more interesting test was that the period 1971–73(II), the period of the major rise in house prices, represents a change or aberration from normal behaviour and that the model can be estimated consistently over the whole period either side of this on the assumption of an unchanged structure. This still has the same characteristic regarding prices as does the hypothesis of a single structural change for the whole of the 1970s but it gives a more comprehensible view of the changes which did occur. On the whole building societies set their interest rates on exactly the same basis throughout the entire period. Housing starts, mortgage advances and mortgage repayments do not show any significant difference in behaviour during the period 1971–73(II). The net change in shares and deposits is better explained by a single equation than the three equation model if the period 1971–73(II) is excluded. This shows that it is behaviour after 1973(II) which exhibits a change as the work of O'Herlihy and Spencer, Hendry and Anderson and the experience here confirm the advantage of separating withdrawals and receipts in the 1950s and 1960s. Mortgage commitments show the weakened price effect which has been mentioned, but also show problems in the determination of the income coefficient. The net acquisition of liquid assets is much better determined showing that the vagaries in behaviour do indeed occur during the period 1971–73(II). The price function on the other hand shows signs of multicollinearity and hence it is difficult to disentangle the results (see Technical Appendix, p. 137). Finally housing completions are shown to follow the lag structure of housing starts more closely with more emphasis on the current period and no significant effect from changes in interest rates or house prices.

In general, therefore, it is inflation and reactions to it which characterize the differences in the behaviour of the model during the 1970s. Building societies do not themselves in general show any significant difference in their behaviour. This does not mean that there were no changes, merely that if there were any they occurred for very much shorter periods. The easiest method of searching for these periods is to examine the pattern of the residuals in the estimated model when it is solved for single period forecasts over the period.

6.2   The Behaviour of Interest Rates

Chapter 4 set out the general pattern to be explained (see Figure 4.8). Interest rates in the early 1970s were historically high, taking bank rate/minimum lending rate as an example, it started at 7 per cent during 1970, fell to 5 per cent in 1972 and rose rapidly reaching a peak of 12.5 per cent in the second quarter of 1974 and only falling slightly thereafter (until the major fall in interest rates in 1977). The building society rates did not follow the fall in 1971, fell temporarily by 0.25 per cent in 1972 as other rates began to rise again, they rose with the general trend in 1973—74 but margins over most competitive rates fell. On a historical basis building society interest rates were relatively favourable during late 1971 to early 1972 and decidedly adverse during late 1973—74. The model largely accepts the relatively favourable period, reducing interest rates less than three months before they actually fell, however, it cannot cope with the really rapid rise in rates during 1973. This is partly because of a too great allowance for stability by the building societies in the changing of interest rates and partly because the pressures on liquidity are not severe with the exception of the first quarter of 1973. Finally the model cannot hold interest rates down during 1974 despite the government loan and they reach a peak in the last quarter of 1974 with the grossed up savings rate at 11.17 per cent and the mortgage rate at 11.32 per cent. This latter implies that the mortgage rate to new borrowers was 11.5 per cent.

The expected effect of this pattern is that building societies would accumulate more funds than usual during 1971—72 and less than usual during late 1973—74. Lending would therefore be facilitated at the beginning of the period and made more difficult at the end. The demand for lending on the other hand would follow approximately the same path, as in the model it is the rate of interest and not the relative rate of interest which affects demand. The model therefore predicts the appropriate cyclical pressure on house prices although at this stage it is not possible to say how much.

6.3   The Inflow of Funds

Section 6.2 noted that relative interest rates would lead us to expect a relative expansion in deposits in 1971–72 and a contraction in later 1973–74. This pattern is in fact observed with the addition of the specially depressed first quarter of 1974. The model however expects a greater inflow of shares and deposits, by £32 million in 1971, £261 million in 1972 and £285 million in 1973, but expects 1974 to be lower by some £214 million. These are errors of 1.6, 11.9, 13.6 and 10.7 per cent respectively, which are fairly substantial in the light of the general close determination of the model. The predicted values also take account of changes in income and the rates of income tax in the estimated equations, although the estimates presented here are from the complete model and so will reflect all variables to some degree. The result of this pattern of the inflow of funds is that we would expect lending to run higher in 1971–73 and lower in 1974, compounding the cycle.

6.4   The Change in Assets – Lending and Liquidity

The predicted pattern of lending does follow what has been expected with over-estimates of £172 million, £222 million and £11 million in 1971–73 and a shortfall of £90 million in 1974. Given the figures for the inflow of funds and the fact that repayments are predicted to within 2 per cent per year this shows that building societies lent about 5 per cent more than might have been expected in 1971 given the inflow of funds, but that in 1973 they held back their lending, and allowed it to run above expectations in 1974. Hence it appears that although societies may have aided the rise in prices in 1972 their lending was actually counter-cyclical in 1973 and 1974 preventing a worse rise and contraction. The predicted over-lending is facilitated by the model's over-prediction of the net acquisition of liquid assets in 1972 and 1973. This gives a larger basis on which to lend in the form of the liquidity ratio. The error involved is not large with a root mean square error of 0.78 for the entire period 1971–74 for the liquidity ratio (LRBS).

Thus as far as building society behaviour is concerned there are two distinct phases. First, interest rates and lending were higher in 1971–72 than might have been expected and second, interest rates were lower than might have been expected in 1973(III)—1974(IV); however, during 1973 lending was lower than might have been expected, compensated by its being higher in 1974. Despite wide fluctuations in inflow the building societies operated within their historical range of liquidity ratios throughout this period although the average value was higher and ratios observed in 1975 were at record levels. This again adds to the suggestion that their behaviour has been relatively cautious.

6.5   The Housing Market

The final task is to link building society behaviour to house prices. The behaviour of the real side of the model should be considered first since the financial variables have been dealt with. As can be seen from Figure 6.1 there is no clear pattern to predicted starts and completions compared with their actual values. The estimates fit well with only a few exceptions, the only discernible features are that in late 1971 to early 1972 both starts and completions are over-predicted and 1974—75

Table 6.1. Actual and Predicted average new house prices

Year		Quarter I	II	III	(1963 = 100) IV
1971	Actual	173	178	191	196
	Predicted	168.7	180.0	186.1	198.7
	% difference	2.5	1.1	2.6	1.4
1972	Actual	206	228	268	292
	Predicted	207.1	220.7	249.8	289.3
	% difference	0.5	3.2	6.8	0.9
1973	Actual	314	329	339	347
	Predicted	312.4	330.9	338.0	344.0
	% difference	0.5	0.6	0.3	0.9
1974	Actual	347	345	354	355
	Predicted	346.5	338.2	342.7	350.9
	% difference	0.1	2.0	3.2	1.1
1975	Actual	365	383	391	
	Predicted	356.9	366.5	391.0	
	% difference	2.2	4.3	0.0	

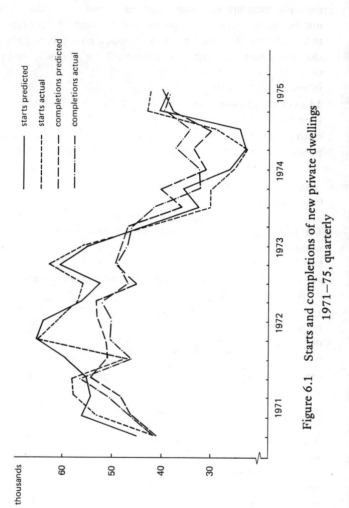

Figure 6.1   Starts and completions of new private dwellings 1971–75, quarterly

starts predicted
starts actual
completions predicted
completions actual

thousands

60

50

30

1971   1972   1973   1974   1975

under-predicted, thus suggesting the expectation of a stronger cycle, which fits in with other previous findings for financial variables.

The final price predictions are equally difficult to analyse. Not surprisingly they are extremely accurate, so much so that a figure would not be illuminating, the values are therefore recorded in Table 6.1 together with the percentage errors. The model does not react fully to extreme changes as is shown clearly in 1972—73. In the first quarter of 1972 prices rise by 10 points which is matched by the prediction; in the second quarter the rise is 22 points while the prediction is only 13.6; in the third quarter they are 40 and 29.1 respectively; while in the fourth they catch up with 24 and 39.5; and in the first quarter of 1973 the two values are back together with an actual rise of 22 points, a predicted rise of 23.1 points.

6.6   Conclusions

The effects of building society behaviour on house prices can now be summarized in a straightforward fashion. On the whole building societies did not respond to the events of the 1970s in an unusual fashion or act in a new way which led to a dramatic rise in prices. There is some limited evidence that the market was slightly out of equilibrium in 1969—70 as building societies had above average liquidity ratios and house prices were relatively depressed compared with incomes and other prices. During 1971 and 1972 building society interest rates moved in favour of depositors and a substantial inflow of funds followed, although if anything rather a smaller inflow than might have been expected. This inflow passed through to mortgage lending in the normal way, although lending was rather more increased than might have been expected. The increase in lending reflects both an increase in demand for as well as supply of mortgages. This lead to an increase in the price of new houses as starts and completions did not pick up as much as might have been expected. In any case new building does not respond quickly to changes in price. As a result the increased demand for housing was not met by a sufficient increase in quantity but by an increase in price. To quite an extent the rise in house prices was self-perpetuating during 1972.

In 1973 the picture changed with building society interest rates becoming less attractive by the end of the year, and the inflow of funds slowing up. At the same time building societies began to lend a little less than might be expected. Interest rates in general soared in 1974 as did the general rate of inflation in prices, but building society interest rates were held down by the end of the year below their expected levels. The first quarter of 1974 saw the three-day week as a result of the miners' strike which reduced incomes and hence there was extremely heavy pressure to reverse the inflation in house prices, which duly occurred in the second quarter of the year, although to a smaller extent than would have been expected.

What this experience shows is that house prices are not stable in the face of cumulative pressures. Several factors combined conveniently to give the system a sufficient push. The sensitivity is not surprising because only small changes in the demand for the stock of housing are impossible to meet through new construction in the short run. A 10 per cent increase for example could only be met by a consistently high level of building for more than a decade. The building societies were certainly a contributory factor in the initial push to inflation with rapidly expanding lending for house purchase. Their actions were not, however, unusual in the context of previous experience. Much of the funds came from contemporaneous inflow aided by very competitive interest rates although some came from a running down of high liquidity levels. Their actions also contributed to the ending of the boom, with the curtailment of lending and the setting of high interest rates. But these actions again could be largely expected from previous behaviour with societies following the general pattern of interest rates. Although lending was perhaps restrained harder than necessary in 1973 it enabled the maintenance of lending at a higher level than would otherwise have been possible in 1974, when pressure on interest rates, not least from the government, kept down the flow of funds.

Fortunately a further test of these hypotheses can be obtained from subsequent movements in the market in 1975—77. Building society lending again expanded rapidly but this time was not faced by a substantial rise in prices. Chapter 7 examines three issues stemming from this experience. Why have house prices not started rising rapidly again? What measures could have been taken to avoid the rise in 1971—73? What measures can be taken to avoid future rises?

7 Prospects and Conclusions

7.1 The Effects of Building Society Behaviour on House Prices in 1976

The end of the last chapter put three questions which the experience of the early 1970s brings forward: (1) why have house prices not started rising rapidly again? (2) what measures could have been taken to avoid the rise in 1971−73? and (3) what measures can be taken to avoid future rises? Each will be considered in turn. All of them involve further simulation with the model developed. One of the great advantages of having a satisfactory model is that unlike Heraclitus we can bathe in the same river twice. The conditions which existed at a particular time period can be replicated and the results of a different set of actions can be seen, or the effect of using the same set of actions under different conditions can be explored. (1) and (3) are examples of this second possibility, while (2) is an example of the first. This of course gives an immediate answer to the question could it all happen again? The answer is clearly yes, if the right circumstances arise and people continue to react in their previous pattern. This of course is a trivial reply and the real concern is over the chance of both similar circumstances and similar reactions occurring.

The first of these two eventualities is easier to deal with since observations are now available on activity during 1975 and 1976 with indications of behaviour in 1977. Already substantial fluctuations in the inflow of funds to building societies have taken place as is shown in Figure 7.1. The inflow increased by 38.4 per cent between the first quarter of 1975 and the first quarter of 1976 and then fell by 54.4 per cent by the end of the year. All the indications are that with building society interest rates falling more slowly than the market as a whole the inflow of funds will build up again rapidly. Lending has shown the

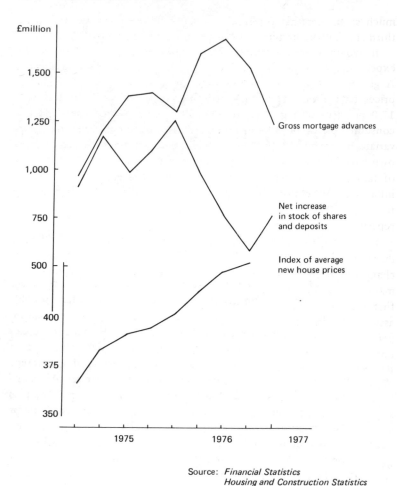

Source: *Financial Statistics*
        Housing and Construction Statistics

Figure 7.1   Building society behaviour and house prices 1975—77

corresponding pattern with a lag as can also be seen from Figure 7.1, with it rising by 74.7 per cent between the first quarter of 1975 and the third quarter of 1976, then falling by 27.7 per cent by the first quarter of 1977. This latter pattern seems to contradict the suggestion that building societies try to stabilize their lending compared with their inflow of funds by taking the worst fluctuations on their liquidity. Since lending has outstripped deposits the liquidity ratio has fallen, so much so in fact that the liquid assets of building societies fell in the third and fourth quarters of 1976 and the first quarter of 1977.

It would therefore appear that there are all the conditions for expecting a corresponding and even more violent cycle in house prices. A glance at Figure 7.1 shows that this has not occurred. Although prices have risen and risen a little unevenly, the total rise was only 17.0 per cent during 1975 and 1976 compared with a rise in general consumer prices of 30.4 per cent. This result emphasizes the multivariate nature of the problem. While building society actions on their own have been potentially destabilizing they have been in the context of falling real incomes, rising unemployment and high rates of general inflation. Furthermore, house prices were still historically high relative to the general price level and the level of incomes, hence there is not a repetition of all the circumstances.

It is perhaps more interesting to look at the behaviour of the model during that period, as it estimates the expected observations given unchanged patterns of behaviour by the protagonists. The results for the major variables are set out in Table 7.1 for two different circumstances, first for single period forecasts during 1976, labelled H1, and second assuming that only the values of the endogenous variables for successive periods are generated by the model labelled H2. In the first place it is noticeable that the model expects higher prices than actually occurred, which in the light of knowledge about building society behaviour during the period suggests that prices have become less responsive to changes. Predicted mortgage advances under both hypotheses suggest a slightly more stable pattern was expected on the basis of previous behaviour than that which actually occurred. This is not, however, true of mortgage commitments under H1 which have a rather sharper pattern. This, therefore, makes it rather more difficult to say whether the observed behaviour really reflects any change in building society behaviour. Looking at the inflow of funds, the predicted interest rate follows the actual pattern very closely, although no reduction is predicted under H2. This not surprisingly results in a higher inflow of funds. (In passing, note that in this model the mortgage rate of interest remains at a lower level.) Combining the inflow and lending behaviour just outlined it is not surprising therefore that the model expects liquidity to run at a higher level than actually occurred.

On the whole the results are fairly closely determined reflecting little change in behaviour during 1976 from previous experience. What change there is suggests that building society behaviour was more

Table 7.1. Prediction for 1976

Variable	Period	Actual value	Estimated H1	% Difference	Estimated H2	% Difference
PH	1976(1)	400.0	404.6	1.2	404.6	1.2
	(2)	413.0	412.1	0.2	417.8	1.0
	(3)	422.0	430.1	1.9	435.6	3.2
	(4)	427.0	436.4	2.2	450.8	5.6
MA	1976(1)	1,322	1,410	6.7	1,410	6.7
	(2)	1,600	1,612	0.7	1,526	4.6
	(3)	1,686	1,614	4.3	1,659	1.6
	(4)	1,526	1,534	0.5	1,643	7.7
NA	1976(1)	808.0	815.7	1.0	815.7	1.0
	(2)	983.0	968.2	1.5	889.7	9.5
	(3)	1,016.0	979.6	3.6	1,000.6	1.5
	(4)	840.0	892.7	6.3	969.7	15.4
IM	1976(1)	10.50	10.56	0.5	10.56	0.5
	(2)	11.37	10.50	7.6	10.52	7.5
	(3)	12.25	10.68	12.8	10.49	14.3
	(4)	11.75	10.57	10.0	10.48	10.8
IS	1976(1)	6.99	6.99	0.0	6.99	0.0
	(2)	6.99	6.99	0.0	6.99	0.0
	(3)	6.49	6.99	7.7	6.99	7.7
	(4)	6.49	6.49	0.0	6.99	7.7
SR	1976(1)	2,723	2,503	8.1	2,503	8.1
	(2)	2,551	2,879	12.9	2,666	4.5
	(3)	2,589	2,659	2.7	2,770	7.0
	(4)	2,476	2,640	6.6	2,847	15.0
SW	1976(1)	1,680	1,726	2.7	1,726	2.7
	(2)	1,865	1,851	0.8	1,891	1.4
	(3)	2,062	2,059	0.2	2,080	0.9
	(4)	2,284	2,225	2.6	2,223	2.7
LR	1976(1)	21.0	22.1	5.1	22.1	5.1
	(2)	20.7	22.4	8.2	22.2	7.3
	(3)	19.9	21.5	7.9	22.1	11.0
	(4)	18.8	20.8	10.4	22.1	17.7
MC	1976(1)	1,522	1,434	5.8	1,434	5.8
	(2)	1,640	1,775	8.2	1,655	0.9
	(3)	1,618	1,477	8.7	1,623	0.3
	(4)	1,326	1,302	1.9	1,579	19.1
HSP	1976(1)	37,970	32,980	13.2	32,980	13.2
	(2)	47,610	47,900	0.6	45,320	4.8
	(3)	44,100	42,360	4.0	41,690	5.5
	(4)	28,950	33,770	16.6	33,350	15.2
HCP	1976(1)	37,940	33,570	11.5	33,570	11.5
	(2)	37,630	41,950	8.6	38,190	1.1
	(3)	39,450	40,510	2.7	39,520	0.2
	(4)	40,070	41,450	3.4	40,800	1.8

unstable than would have been expected, and that prices were less sensitive to upward pressures than they had been previously. From this basis it could be argued that the housing market has learnt from the experiences of 1971–73 and is now less likely to move into rapid inflation. Building societies on the other hand appear to have increasingly volatile behaviour. To quite some extent this is due to the increasingly volatile environment, in particular the size and rapidity of fluctuations in the market rates of interest and the resulting fluctuations in net new shares and deposits.

Before leaving this section recall that the close determination of these predictions outside the sample period of this estimated model is itself a vindication of the specification and estimates obtained.

7.2   The Control of House Prices

In view of the outcry which accompanied the rapid rise in house prices it is clear that many people would have preferred the rise not to have taken place in the way it did. Clearly it is virtually impossible for any of the individual buyers and sellers of houses to have much effect on house prices, with the exception of some large construction firms. The main ordered influences on the market can hence only come from two sources, the building societies and the government. The explicit joint control which societies exercise comes through the interest rates agreed by the Council of the Building Societies Association. Lending by individual societies is almost entirely a matter for their own judgement. It is therefore only possible for the building society movement to influence the market as a whole at discrete monthly intervals and then with a time lag, especially in the case of changes in the mortgage rate of interest. Under stable circumstances this is not particularly important, but under fluctuating market rates of interest this procedure will be positively destabilizing. If rates of interest are rising societies will tend to lag behind and hence lose funds, while if they are falling the lag will cause them to become highly competitive and hence gain funds rapidly. Quite the opposite pressure exists for lending. The demand for funds will not slacken as quickly as the inflow of funds and the cyclical pattern will be emphasized.

It would appear, therefore, that a solution might be the more frequent assessment of building society interest rates, but this exceeds the constraint of practicality. It is always awkward to organize the coherent behaviour of a group of independent concerns, and in any case there are considerable costs to changing interest rates and hence a justifiable aversion to doing so. The only alternative stabilizing policy is that which has actually been adopted by the societies, namely to have a higher liquidity ratio. This provides a greater buffer between the inflow of funds and the outflow of lending and hence enables more of the cyclical fluctuation in the inflow to be absorbed. However, on the basis of the very limited evidence available, it appears that in fact this extra liquidity has not been used quite as much as might have been expected, although it permitted a 7.8 per cent reduction in liquid assets between 1976(II) and 1977(I) while mortgage assets rose by 12.3 per cent. The only remaining constraint that societies could impose, would be to make limits on the sizes of the change in lending which they are prepared to see in any one time. This of course would be in opposition to ordinary commercial criteria and hence is unlikely to operate.

The building society movement is thus not well placed to try to prevent further fluctuations in house prices if there is no change in the degree of fluctuations in the economy as a whole. This might imply that the onus for alleviating pressures on house prices lies with the government. This is true in the sense that the government influences the major economic aggregates of incomes and prices, and has not made a striking success of doing so over the past few years. It does not, however, necessarily imply that the government should intervene to control house prices and building society lending directly. It seems fairly clear that government intervention to influence building society interest rates is not necessarily beneficial. If pressure is used to hold rates down below economic levels this merely sharpens the downturn in lending, makes it difficult for people to move house and exaggerates the reaction to rectify the situation when the pressure has been removed in order to restore liquidity. The use of loans at favourable rates of interest is, however, stabilizing as it reduces the pressure on the outflow while it is outstanding and holds back lending while it is being repaid. It does, however, mean that the government is explicitly subsidizing home ownership.

Further direct intervention is available from government finance for house purchase or home construction, whether in the public or private sectors. Again this can be used in a counter-cyclical fashion as well as the continuing aim of helping those who either cannot afford to buy their own homes (through local authority housing) or who have problems in finding initial payments (option mortgages, loans for first-time buyers, etc.). There are, of course, major problems in establishing coherent housing policies between sectors if short-run measures are used, as is noted in Mayes and Stafford (1977).

Hadjimatheou (1976) considers the effects on house prices of varying the standard rate of income tax, although he does not take into account the fact that it will affect personal disposable income as well. For this reason we have not considered what the explicit effect would be on our model, but it is clear that this could be used as a policy instrument. Naturally explicit changes in the tax rate to affect house prices are not expected but there will be implications of changes for other reasons. If the tax rate rises the direct demand for new housing falls as disposable incomes fall. This fall is alleviated because of the existence of tax relief on mortgage interest. At the same time the inflow of funds into building societies will be cut so that the pressure on prices from mortgage lending will be reduced. However, if the composite rate of tax paid by societies is unchanged building society deposits will become relatively more attractive to income taxpayers.

Thus in conclusion it can be said that the government can help to counteract the reaction of house prices to fluctuations in building society lending, either by aiding building societies to stabilize the rate of growth of lending through providing loans, or by intervening directly by encouraging local authority and new town building both for rent and sale in a counter-cyclical fashion or by encouraging direct lending for house purchase and construction.

These conclusions apply to both the future and the past, but the two cases are rather different. The rise in 1971—73 occurred when societies had a surplus of funds and had not yet experienced a severe shortage as in 1973—74, hence it was a matter of affecting the initial upturn, rather than trying to decrease the amplitude of continuing fluctuations which appears to be the current and future problem. The initial prevailing disequilibrium in mortgage and housing markets in 1970 was not of such dimensions that action could have reasonably been expected, except in so far as the supply of new housing had fallen substantially below its 1964 peak. A slightly better timing of interest rate movements by building societies would have reduced the impetus and subsequent pressure to some degree, but there is no single readily identifiable policy or behavioural change which could have been made which would have avoided the rapid inflation. The cycle was very short, and given the way that our model shows how inflation feeds on itself a substantial injection to the system for only six months is quite sufficient to set the whole process in motion.

Avoiding subsequent fluctuations is rather easier to manage because we have the benefit of hindsight, and hence can identify the signals of an impending rise rather more clearly. Nevertheless the experience of 1976 suggests that a new cycle is not likely to be controlled, and that a second burst of price rises only failed to occur because some of the conditions were not present, not because any steps were taken to avoid it. The only reassuring element is that the market now appears to be somewhat less sensitive than it was in 1971–72. It remains to be seen what will happen if house prices fall for another two years relative to the general price level, wages begin to rise after being held down by the 'social contract' and building societies experience a rapid inflow of funds from a change in market rates of interest, but experience suggests that house prices will rise fairly rapidly again. The greatest likelihood is of course for the various events to be out of phase and for house prices to rise far more in line with the general rate of inflation with continuing cycles in lending. In the longer run it can be expected that the economy as a whole will pick up and the construction industry will recover from its current low ebb, which taken together also suggest a return to more steadily rising house prices as demand increases, but supply increases also with a short lag. Nevertheless in common with many sectors it will be several years before we can hope for a return to the more orderly progress of the 1950s and 1960s.

Technical Appendix

Purpose and Contents

This appendix is divided into four main parts. The first gives the definitions of the variables used in the book and their statistical sources. The remaining three are concerned with statistical and econometric problems which are encountered in modelling the workings of the building society sector and the market for new housing. The first of these three sections concerns the estimation and specification of the structure of the model and hence explains the general problems encountered and the reasons for the decisions we have taken. The second section is then concerned with points of detail relating to individual equations. Finally, the last section covers the problems involved in the simulation of the model, both over the data period and beyond.

A.1. LIST OF VARIABLES AND DEFINITIONS

ALI	Building society holdings of cash and investments	£million	FS
AM	Stock of building society mortgages outstanding	£million	FS
AO	Stock of other assets held by building societies	£million	FS
ATOT	Total assets of building societies	£million	FS
BR	Bank rate/minimum lending rate	%	FS
CC	Cost of new construction in Great Britain (excluding repairs and maintenance)	1954 = 100	HC
D3	Dummy variable for severe winter in 1963	1963(I) = 1.0	
D4	Dummy variable for Betterment Levy	1967(I,II) = 1.0	
D5	Dummy variable for three-day week	1974(I) = 1.0	
D6	Dummy variable for parameter shifts under inflation	1971(I)—76(I) = 1.0	
D7	Dummy variable for parameter shifts under inflation	1971(I)—73(III) = 1.0	
D8	Dummy variable for reaction to D3	1963(II) = 1.0	

D9	Dummy variable for severe winter in 1969	1969(I) = 1.0	
GL	Government loan to hold down interest rates	£million	FS
HCO	Completions of new houses in non-private sector	no.	HC
HCP	Completions of new houses in private sector	no.	HC
HP	Stock of houses, private sector	no.	HC
HSP	Starts of new private houses	no.	HC
ICR	Interest credited to accounts by building societies	£million	FS
ID	Time-trend	1955(I) = 1, 1976(II) = 86	
IM	Rate of interest on building society mortgages	%	FS
IS	Weighted average of building society share and deposit rates	%	FS
ITC	Yield on 2.5% consols	%	FS
LAHS	Sales of local authority houses	no.	HC
LAR	Local authority rents	1962(III) = 100	HC
LR	Building society liquidity ratio	%	FS
M	Marriages in Great Britain	1,000	AA
MA	Gross new mortgage advances by building societies	£million	FS
MC	New mortgage commitments by building societies	£million	FS
ME	Lending for house purchase by other financial institutions	£million	FS
MR	Repayment of principal to building societies	£million	FS
N	Population of UK	1,000	MD
NA	Net new mortgage advances by building societies	£million	FS
OMC	Outstanding mortgage commitments by building societies (end of period)	£million	FS
PC	Implicit deflator of consumers expenditure	1963 = 100	ET
PH	Price of new houses	1963 = 100	HC
Qi	Seasonal dummy variable for quarter i		
RR	Reserve ratio of building societies		FS
SC	Closures and demolitions, private sector	no.	HC
SD	Stock of shares and deposits with building societies	£million	FS
SR	Receipts of new shares and deposits by building societies	£million	FS
SW	Withdrawals of shares and deposits with building societies	£million	FS

T	Composite rate of tax agreed on interest payments by building societies	%	FSS
Y	Personal disposable income	£million	ET
YT	Standard rate of income tax	%	ET
−i	Denotes a lag of i quarters		

(AA   Annual Abstract of Statistics)
(ET   Economic Trends)
(FS   Financial Statistics) (F.S.S. F.S. Supplement)
(HC   Housing and Construction Statistics (previously
         Housing Statistics and Construction Statistics
         separately))
(MD   Monthly Digest of Statistics)

All other variables not defined here are defined by the relationships of the model in Table 5.1, pp. 79–80.

A.2   The Structure and Estimation of the Model

A.2.1 Estimation Method

The model specified in Table 5.2 is clearly simultaneous. Its time series nature and the hypotheses of partial adjustment suggest that it will have a complex autoregressive structure. It is quite likely that the autoregressive processes are not independent between equations, hence an estimation method is required which will take account of all these possibilities together. At first glance Full Information Maximum Likelihood (FIML) looks a suitable candidate for an estimation method and several initial attempts were made to use it. There are a number of drawbacks to doing this. First the size of the model with fifteen simultaneous equations and up to eighty-four observations on each of over fifty variables makes estimation lengthy and tedious. In practice the model was divided into sections and each section estimated in this way. Second there are non-linear constraints between equations which are difficult to incorporate into the estimation. (They are in fact impossible to incorporate in the package programme which was used, and it would be an unrealistic expenditure of time to develop a specific FIML programme for this particular model.) Last the FIML results obtained did not in many cases vary widely from the more restricted estimates actually used.

It was, therefore, decided that rather than using different estimation methods for various parts of the model with in effect less than full information that a single coherent approach was preferable. This involved restricting the autoregressive process to first order and using instrumental variables to take account of the simultaneity. This procedure is similar to that described in Godfrey (1973) although it used a much more inefficient convergence routine than his Powell (1964) algorithm. There are obvious worries that the elimination of higher orders of autoregression might lead to inefficient estimates, and where possible equations were rerun using the Hendry (1972) RALS routine to examine higher orders. On the whole this suggested that a first order process was sufficient, although in some cases there was evidence of fourth order autocorrelation as might be expected from a quarterly model, see Hendry and Anderson (1976) and Wallis and Thomas (1971). It would have been preferable perhaps to re-estimate with first and fourth order autocorrelation alone, but this was not possible with the computer programmes which were readily available.

The choice of instruments to be included in the various equations was made purely on the basis of the main determinants of the endogenous variables including lagged values where appropriate. The number of degrees of freedom permitted the inclusion of up to a dozen instruments without any loss of determination. (In the case of equations which were independent and did not show autocorrelation OLS results are shown in Table 5.2. Otherwise if no coefficient of autocorrelation is reported instrumental variables alone were used. The existence of an autoregressive relation can be examined by a simple χ^2 test, Hendry (1972).)

A.2.2 The Structure of the Model

Although the general structure of the model was established in the form wanted, two constraints were accepted on the final specification. The first constraint is that imposed by the data and the second that imposed by the functional form. The data constraint largely occurs because it is not always possible to obtain values for the exact variables required and therefore it is necessary either to resort to the use of a proxy variable or variables or to respecify the model. The main areas of data deficiency concern the divisions between new and existing housing and between owner-occupied and privately rented property, although there are also some discrepancies with interest rates.

Taking the division between new and existing housing first, this has most effect on the specification of building society lending. Only a part of building society lending is for the purchase of new housing, but it is not possible to get a full breakdown of commitments and advances until 1969 which gives too short an estimation period to be useful. However, it is not immediately clear that this mis-specification is an important disadvantage. Although building societies exhibit a preference for lending on recently built properties it is not clear that their lending on new properties follows any strikingly different pattern. There is however, a constraint on lending on new properties in that the number of loans cannot exceed the number of new properties sold in a particular time period (although there may be some time lag between purchase and the receipt of a building society advance, probably covered by a bridging loan from a bank, which will cause discrepancies between the figures). Hence if building societies lend large sums of money this inevitably results in an expansion of lending on existing housing rather than new housing. The pressure on prices, therefore, in an upward direction, actually occurs on the market for existing housing as expansion can occur in the form of increased turnover. The validity of the model therefore rests on the closeness of the relation between existing and new house prices, that an expansion in lending on existing houses affects their price and this in turn affects the price of new houses as a very close substitute. In this case therefore although the intervening links are missed out and new house prices related to total lending directly, there is actually a better specification of the relation being sought than considering lending for new dwellings alone. The real drawback is that satisfactory data on the sales and prices of all houses which pass through the market cannot be obtained. The source which shows the figures for both number and value of advances and commitments on new and existing housing most clearly is *Fact and Figures* published by the Building Societies Association, rather than the official *CSO Financial Statistics* which give rather shorter series (from the same source).

The division between owner-occupied and privately rented property is a rather more difficult problem. The statistics for construction distinguish between the private and public sectors. It is not clear how this construction in the private sector is distributed between owner-occupied and rented property, although there are estimates of the stock from survey data. The distinction is important as building societies normally only lend for purchase by owner-occupiers (strictly to those who say they will be owner-occupiers). Further, building societies are not so keen to lend on second rather than first homes. So while building society lending relates primarily to owner-occupied main homes, the construction statistics refer to a wider group of dwellings.

Another source of discrepancy is the distinction between Great Britain and the UK, explained very clearly in Whitehead (1974). This text has opted where possible to deal with Great Britain, as Northern Ireland is subject to special factors over much of the estimation period and especially from 1969 onwards. Not only is the pattern of construction, closure and prices different, but building society lending is also on a slightly different basis. Hewitt and Thom (1977) show very clearly that while in 1966 the ratio of the stock of shares and deposits generated in Northern Ireland to mortgage liabilities on property there was 0.31 by 1975 it had risen to 1.09. Thus instead of the building society movement channelling funds from the rest of the country into Northern Ireland the position has just been reversed. It is thus helpful to the accuracy of the analysis to try to exclude Northern Ireland, although since the large majority of building societies operating in Northern Ireland are based in the rest of the United Kingdom the behaviour in Northern Ireland will affect their behaviour elsewhere.

The second major constraint mentioned at the beginning of this section was the choice of functional form. There are many straightforward functional forms which are available and can be estimated readily. The main requirement is merely that given a relation of the form:

$$Y = f(X, E) \tag{1}$$

where E is a matrix of errors that E should have a form with manageable statistical properties, so that the estimators of f can be fully useful. Thus from a purely statistical point of view it does not matter very much if, say, a first difference, a logarithmic, semi-logarithmic or a proportionate form is chosen instead of a linear one. However, substantial practical problems for estimation may be posed in a simultaneous system if we choose too many different forms. In particular there would be problems with cross equation constraints and the appropriate use of instruments. All the four alternative functional forms just mentioned are used in one or other of the models of housing and building society markets have been considered, and in fact two of them have been used here, first difference and logarithmic. On the whole the linear specification is justified, although in the case of the inflow of shares and deposits an improved specification suggested by Foster (1975) was noted. It is, however, usually a little difficult to give a precise explanation of why a particular functional form is preferred. A number of criteria can be used: the standard error of estimate, the size, sign and significance of the coefficients, the accuracy of prediction etc., but it is not really possible to say how much better one specification is than another, especially since the true relation can never be known. This study, therefore, has examined both linear and other specifications when there appeared to be a choice, according to those criteria. In no case did it appear that a linear specification gave seriously inferior results, and in some cases it was clearly the best specification. Thus while if it were possible to write an estimation programme to account for a wide variety of specifications within this simultaneous framework the resulting estimates would be improved, the degree of distortion obtained by linearizing does not seem likely to be serious. This conclusion cannot, of course, be certain as estimation on a piecemeal basis is not a proper substitute for estimating the full system.

A.3   The Individual Estimated Equations

A model of this size naturally throws up most of the well known problems in econometrics, and where possible conventional solutions have been used. For ease of reference, this section takes each equation in the order given in Table 5.1 and considers the specific problems if any relating to it. The subsections end with the same number as the equation to which they refer.

A.3.1 The Average Price of New Houses

This equation presents two main problems, the first of which is stability and the second multicollinearity. The results reported in Neuberger and Nichol (1976) show that by appropriate choice of estimation period it is possible to obtain a coefficient for the lagged dependent variable greater than unity, although not significantly greater. This would result in an unstable model. The results we obtained gave values very close to unity, but always below it (except with longer lag structures which had offsetting values to avoid the problem. Being close to instability has worrying repercussions as any changes take a very long time before their effect on the system dies out. Neuberger and Nichol (1976, p. 45) justify their findings on the ground that it reflects 'we feel the reinvestment of capital gain and expectations of price change'. More precisely that, certainly during the period 1971—73 and possibly elsewhere, people's reactions do mean that, in the absence of countervailing pressures, inflation is an explosive process. The practical counter is of course first that there are countervailing pressures which in fact stop the system getting out of hand indefinitely and second that the model is only to explain a short-run phenomenon and hence the properties of its long-run equilibrium are not of prime importance. These two provisions also apply to our own results even though the model does converge to a long-run equilibrium with fixed values of the exogenous variables and no random disturbances.

The existence of multicollinearity poses the usual dilemma for the investigator, should he sacrifice some of the variables in which he is interested or the identification of their individual effects. The standard procedure has been followed in this book (see for example Maddala (1977) for an exposition) of examining the inverse of the matrix of simple correlation coefficients of the determining variables. This helps to identify the collinear set from the appropriate diagonal and off-diagonal elements. If it is felt that the model has been specified very well, purely statistical methods could be used to overcome the problems of near singularity in the inversion procedure (the matrix inverted is not of course just the variance-covariance matrix of X). The possibilities in common use are regression on the first few principle components and ridge regression, but neither of these is particularly attractive in this case. Since the specification of some of the variables is an attempt to capture the effects of the number of potential households and the effects of other parts of the housing market, a simple separable specification is preferable to a collinear one. It is only if we are really convinced that the collinear specification is undoubtedly correct and the simple specification is much inferior that we should persevere. In this case it is more important to try to disentangle the particular economic effects than to concentrate on, say, minimizing the standard error of estimate. It is clear from the final result that although the equation used may be simple and exclude important variables such as population and local authority rents it does explain average new house prices extremely closely.

A.3.2 Completions

The two problems this equation presented, the form of the distributed lag on starts and the price adjustment term have already been noted in the text. It is, however, necessary to amplify the problem of estimating the form of the distributed lag a little. The choice to be made in establishing the form of a distributed lag

$$Y = \frac{A(L)}{B(L)} X \qquad (2)$$

(where L is the lag operator and A and B give the parameters of the lag distributions on X and Y) is over the degree of constraint to be placed on the estimation of the parameters. Clearly some limits must be imposed on either the form or the length of the lag distribution if it is to be estimated. In this particular case it is reasonably certain that from a purely technical point of view a very large proportion of houses started are completed within about a couple of years, hence the constraint that parameters after eight periods should be zero is not unreasonable. It is difficult to say what exact shape the lag distribution should have except in so far as in general houses are completed sooner rather than later with a modal and mean lag of around two to three quarters. The more complex the general form of the lag the more difficult it is to specify and the greater the temptation to leave the form unconstrained and hope that problems of collinearity in estimation are not too important. The general specification therefore permitted a seven-period distributed lag on starts with a single general first order autoregressive parameter for the equation as a whole. Despite the drawbacks from constraint, imposing a third order Almon lag had the most satisfactory results although with the proviso noted about its shape, which may be accounted for partly by the seasonal structure of the industry.

A.3.5 Mortgage Commitments

This equation presented some of the hardest specification problems, as it was necessary to show the constraint of liquidity and reserves on lending plans. It is readily arguable that the choice of linearity is a poor representation of reality and that either the Hendry and Anderson (1976) quadratic loss approach or a dis-equilibrium model, perhaps along the lines of Hadjimatheou (1976) should have been adopted. The existence of collinearity and instability among the parameters confirms the worry of mis-specification. However, attempts to increase the cost of disequilibrium or introduce a variable target value of liquidity round which to base the disequilibrium did not overcome the problems. Therefore, simplicity was opted for on the grounds that the nature of the specification was then clear and that drawbacks of the approach were then more obvious and easier to allow for in simulation.

A.3.9 and 10 The Inflow of Funds

The specification used is a conscious linearization of Foster's (1975) relation, again chosen for simplicity. Since a price expectations series for the whole of the estimation period was not available Foster's results could not be reproduced exactly. The resulting respecification using his general form did not appear to give any very appreciable improvement. Collinearity was also experienced from including a third interest rate variable. The resulting equations do, however, require further refinement as they tend to over predict the inflow of funds to building societies from shares and deposits when the model is simulated.

A.3.11 Interest Credited to Accounts

This relation is intended as a purely technical estimate as it is only data in-adequacies which prevent us calculating this variable exactly. A simple linear or log-linear specification shows striking heteroscedasticity in the residuals. This has two causes. First the inaccuracy of the relation does indeed increase with the value of the interest credited and second the seasonal pattern also increases in amplitude over time. This has been overcome by in effect splitting the estimation period in two. In the first part (up to 1967) a simple lag is used to characterize the model, and in the second seasonal constants whose values increase over time are added. The two periods each have homoscedastic error variances on the basis of Chow tests.

A.4   The Simulation of the Model

There are three major issues which need to be explained concerning the simulated model. The first concerns the structural stability of the model outside the 1950s and 1960s, the second concerns the choice of the method of simulation and the third the evaluation of the results. Beginning with the structural stability of the model, it was noted with some concern in Chapter 5 that the striking behaviour observed during the 1970s could be the result of a structural change or changes in human or institutional behaviour during that period. Two possibilities were suggested, first that there was a single structural change which took place in 1971 and second that the structural change was not permanent and ended in the third quarter of 1973. There are two ways of dealing with this, the first is to incorporate dummy variables which permit a shift in the parameters during part of the estimation period, and the second is to see how well the model forecasts during the period when the shift is thought to have taken place on the basis of the rest of the data period.

Both of these methods were used. In the first place it is possible to test for the existence of any structural shift by the use of an appropriate Chow test and to look at the importance of the change in any individual parameter by means of the t statistics. In some cases, the explanation of mortgage commitments in particular, the number of degrees of freedom becomes very small and the results are of no great value. The second method of considering the validity of forecasts by a simple χ^2 test is a more general test of parameter stability and does not require the identification of the nature of the structural changes. This procedure thus has the advantage of identifying more complex changes and the disadvantage of neither specifying nor suggesting the nature of the solution to the structural change. It was therefore useful to consider the results from both methods.

The simulation model was solved in each time period by a simple iterative process. The equations were ordered so that as far as possible endogenous variables were not included on the righthand side of equations until an estimate had been obtained of their value. Where this was not possible actual values of endogenous variables were used as starting values and the sequence was solved iteratively until a maximum proportionate error criterion was met (accuracy of one in one thousand). The method seemed invariant to reasonable changes in the starting values, and converged extremely quickly (reflecting the level of simultaneity and high degree of determination of the model). There are other more efficient methods available, but given the simplicity and efficiency of the method used there was no point in bothering to try to implement them.

Finally the evaluation of the forecasts themselves presented no unusual problems, but it was necessary to bear in mind that a simple RMSE criterion alone is not sufficient information. Not only does the model seem to predict better by RMSE comparison with naive models (simple trends or constant values), but the time paths often exhibit the appropriate directions of change in succeeding periods. There are specific non-parametric tests available to consider these results (see, Pindyck and Rubinfeld (1975)) for example. We have therefore looked in the text at the time paths and evaluated the forecasts accordingly. In conclusion note that the accuracy of the forecasts over quite long periods shows the satisfactory behaviour of the model albeit that some of the simulation period lies within the estimation period.

A.5 Postscript

No attempt has been made in this appendix to regurgitate standard results, there are a large number of econometrics textbooks which cover the ground clearly. Any individual points which are not clear (Chow tests for example) can be looked up in say Maddala (1977), and that book with perhaps Dhrymes (1970), Goldberger (1964), Malinvaud (1970) and Theil (1971) should cover all the problems in a way satisfactory to the reader. A quick introduction to the subject can be obtained from Mayes and Mayes (1976) and Stewart (1976) both of which use only a very limited level of mathematics.

References

Alberts, W.W. (1962) 'Business Cycles, Residential Constructions and the Mortgage Market' *Journal of Political Economy* (June).

Artis, M.J., Kiernan, E. and Whitley, J.D. (1975) 'The Effects of Building Society Behaviour on Housing Investment' in Parkin, J.M. and Nobay, A.E. (eds.) *Contemporary Issues in Economics* Manchester University Press, ch. 2.

Ashton, R.K. (1974) 'The Housing Market' *National Westminster Bank Review* August.

Boléat, M. (1976) 'House Prices and the Housing Market' *Housing Review* October.

Building Societies Association (1975 +) *Facts and Figures* London.

Building Societies Association (1976) *Evidence to the Housing Finance Review* London.

Byatt (1975) comment on Artis *et al.* (1975) in Parkin and Nobay (1975).

Clayton, G., Dodds, J.C., Driscoll, M.J. and Ford, J.L. (1975) 'The Portfolio and Debt Behaviour of British Building Societies' *SUERF* paper no. 16A.

Cmnd 6851 (1977) *Housing Policy Review* (Report and Technical Volume of 3 parts) London, HMSO.

Cooper, M.H. and Stafford, D.C. (1975) 'A Note on Fair Rents' *Social and Economic Administration*.

Dhrymes, P.J. (1970) *Econometrics* New York, Harper & Row.

Duffy, M. (1970) 'A Model of UK Private Investment in Dwellings' Econometric Forecasting Unit, London Graduate School of Business Studies, discussion paper no. 18.

Evans, M.K. (1969) *Macroeconomic Activity* New York, Harper & Row.

Fair, R.C. (1973) 'Monthly Housing Starts' in Ricks (1973).

Fair, R.C. and Jaffee, D.M. (1972) 'Methods of Estimation for Markets in Disequilibrium' *Econometrica* May.

Foster, J. (1975) 'The Demand for Building Society Shares and Deposits: 1961—73' *Oxford Bulletin of Economics and Statistics* vol. 37 pt 4 pp. 319-41.

Ghosh, D. (1974) *The Economics of Building Societies*, Farnborough (Hants), Saxon House.

Ghosh, D. and Parkin, J.M. (1972) 'A Theoretical and Empirical Analysis of the Portfolio: Debt and Interest Rate Behaviour of Building Societies' *Manchester School* September pp. 231-44.

Godfrey, L.G. (1973) 'Some Comments on the Estimation of the Lipsey—Parkin Inflation Model' in Parkin, J.M. and Sumner, M.T. (eds.) *Incomes Policy and Inflation* Manchester, Manchester University Press 1973.

Goldberger, A.S. (1964) *Econometric Theory* London, John Wiley and Sons.

Gough, T.J. (1972), 'Determinants of Fluctuations in Private Housing Investment' *Applied Economics* June.

Guttentag, J.M. (1961) 'The Short Cycle in Residential Construction' *American Economic Review* vol. 51 no. 3 June.

Hadjimatheou, G. (1976) *Housing and Mortgage Markets* Farnborough (Hants), Saxon House.

Hall and Hitch (1939) 'Price Theory and Economic Behaviour' *Oxford Economic Papers*.

Harrington, R.L. (1972) 'Housing — Supply and Demand' *National Westminster Bank Review* May.

Hendry, D.F. (1972) 'User's Manual for RALS' London School of Economics, mimeo, July.

Hendry, D. and Anderson, G.J. (1976) 'Testing Dynamic Specification in Small Simultaneous Systems: an application to a model of building society behaviour in the United Kingdom' London School of Economics, Econometrics Programme, discussion paper no. A4.

HM Treasury (1977) *HM Treasury Macroeconomic Model Technical Manual 1977* London February.

Hewitt, V.N. and Thom, D.R. (1977) 'An Econometric Model of Building Society Behaviour in Northern Ireland' The Queen's University of Belfast, Working Papers in Economics, occasional paper no. 9.

Holmans, A.E. (1970) 'A Forecast of the Effective Demand for Housing in Great Britain in the 1970s' in *Social Trends* no. 1 London, HMSO.

Kalchbrenner, J.H. (1973) 'Summary of the Current Financial Intermediary, Mortgage and Housing Sectors of the SSRC—MIT—Penn Model' in Ricks (1973).

London Graduate School of Business Studies (1976) 'The London Business School Quarterly Econometric Model of the United Kingdom Economy: Relationships in the Basic Model as at April 1976' Econometric Forecasting Unit, appendix to discussion paper no. 34.

Maddala, G.S. (1977) *Econometrics* New York, McGraw-Hill.

Malinvaud, E. (1970) *Statistical Methods of Econometrics* Amsterdam, North Holland 2nd edn.

Maisel, S. (1963) 'A Theory of Fluctuations in Residential Construction Starts' *American Economic Review* June.

Mayes, A.C. and Mayes, D.G. (1976) *Introductory Economic Statistics* London, John Wiley and Sons.

Mayes, D.G. and Stafford, D.C. (1977) 'The Effects of Inconsistent Government Policy in the UK Housing Market' *The Bankers Magazine*.

Needleman, L. (1965) *The Economics of Housing* London, Staples Press.

Neuberger, H.L.I. and Nichol, B.M. (1976) *The Recent Course of Land and Property Prices and the Factors Underlying it* Department of the Environment, research report no. 4.

O'Herlihy, C. St.J. and Spencer, J.E. (1972) 'Building Societies' Behaviour, 1955—70' *National Institute Economic Review* no. 61 August.

Paige, D.C. (1965) 'Housing' in Beckerman, W. *et al. The British Economy in 1975* London, Cambridge University Press.

Parkin, J.M. and Norbay, A.R. (eds.) (1975) *Contemporary Problems in Economics* London, Heinemann.

Pindyck, R.S. and Rubinfeld, D.L. (1975) *Econometric Models and Economic Forecasts* New York, McGraw-Hill.

Powell, M.J.D. (1964) 'An Efficient Method for Finding the Minimum of a Function of Several Variables Without Calculating Derivatives' *Computer Journal* vol. 7 pp. 155—62.

Redmond, J. (1974) 'The UK Housing Market' *National Westminster Bank Review* November.

Renton, G.A. (ed.) (1975) *Modelling the Economy* London, Heinemann.

Revell, J. (1973a) *The British Financial System* London, Macmillan.

Revell, J. (1973b) 'UK Building Societies' University College of North Wales, research paper fin. 5.

Ricks, R.B. (ed.) (1973) *National Housing Models* Lexington, D.C. Heath & Co.

Riley, C.J. (1974) 'A Model of Building Society Behaviour' HM Treasury mimeo.

Stewart, J. (1976) *Introduction to Econometrics* Manchester, Manchester University Press.

Theil, H. (1971) *Textbook of Econometrics* Amsterdam, North Holland.

Wallis, K.F. and Thomas, J.J. (1971) 'Seasonal Variations in Regression Analysis' *Journal of the Royal Statistical Society* series A vol. 134 pt 1 pp. 57-72.

Whitehead, C.M.E. (1974) *The UK Housing Market: an econometric model* Farnborough (Hants), Saxon House.

Index